THE

Pathways to Our
Innermost Being

Pietro Archiati

TEMPLE LODGE
London

Translated by Pauline Wehrle

Temple Lodge Publishing
51 Queen Caroline Street
London W6 9QL

Published by Temple Lodge 1998

Originally published in German in 1997 under the title *Die Weltreligionnen, Wege des Menschen zu sich selbst* by Verlag am Goetheanum, Dornach, Switzerland in 1993

A catalogue record for this book is available from the British Library

ISBN 1 902636 01 5

Cover: art by Fergus Anderson; layout by Sevak Gulbekian
Typeset by DP Photosetting, Aylesbury, Bucks
Printed and bound in Great Britain by Cromwell Press Limited, Trowbridge, Wiltshire

CONTENTS

PREFACE

In recent years I have had an opportunity in various places to discuss, in courses, seminars and lectures, the evolution of religions in the history of humankind. In this volume the reader will find the essence of that work put into a form in which I have deliberately preserved something of the spontaneity of a lecture. Rudolf Steiner's spiritual science has something to say about religions which cannot be found elsewhere. According to this, every human being experiences, in the succession of events, each religion as a stage in the process of becoming human. A person will experience the turning-point of time when he transforms *within his own being* the various religions that follow one after another — or even conflict with one another — into one of co-operating together or mutually supporting one another. For the harmony of all the religions is founded in human nature itself.

So we have to distinguish clearly between religion and individuality. No one must be identified with his present religion — and this also applies to nationality or race. Religion, too, is a sheath, and in the course of ages each human being moves on from one sheath to another. No single individual is a Christian or a Muslim or a Hindu, any more than an individual — as a human being — can be black or white.

Looked at in this way the unity of all religions acquires quite a new significance. It does not consist of what the various religions 'teach' or 'have to say' in common. The theory they expound is of secondary importance. The essence of a religion is in what it makes of a human being. And the actual unity of all religions is the creative product they have combined to make, namely, the *human being*

himself as the synthesis of all the religious paths which he
has trodden in the course of his long evolution.

And what of the founders of the religions themselves: the
Buddha, Krishna, Moses, Zarathustra...? True spiritual
science asks not only what they said and did *in their time* but
also: where is the Buddha *today*, where is Zarathustra *today*?
What is the Buddha telling people *now*, how is he working
now among humankind? Is he saying and doing exactly the
same things as before, although humankind has radically
changed? And how do the spiritually godlike beings of all
the religions relate to one another *today*? If we take the
reality of *evolution* seriously, then at any given time the true
and best religion is the one which brings to human beings
what is right for that time. If the right religion for today is
the harmonizing of all religions in the heart of each human
being, is this harmonizing process not a reflection of the
heavenly harmony among all those godlike beings and
God-inspired human beings who have bestowed upon
humankind the various religions?

May these pages contribute not only to an understanding
of the religions but above all to an understanding of human
beings among themselves. For it is mutual understanding
alone which can serve as a foundation for true tolerance and
for the mutual love of all people.

1
RELIGION OR RELIGIONS?

When we consider the phenomenon of the religious life in the evolution of humanity we have first of all to ask what 'religion' means altogether. The word comes from Latin and means something like 're-establishing a connection'. It draws our attention to the fact that in the course of evolution a separation has come about — a separation from our original heavenly home — and that human beings are endeavouring to revoke this separation by 're-establishing a connection'.

The underlying thought, which occurs in many variations in all religions and also in all mythologies, is this. In the beginning humanity was quite different from what it is today and has undergone great changes in the course of evolution. Initially the human being was united with the Godhead and lived in 'Paradise'. He lived in the bosom of the Godhead, had not yet become separate, and was not yet capable of experiencing himself as an independent being. It was as though he were still a thought of the Godhead himself — just as a thought which a person has today does not immediately acquire an existence of its own but remains part of the person himself, a manifestation of his inner being.

This original human condition was overcome and left behind. Humankind began to separate from the Godhead. This separation is a process involving long aeons of time. The human race gradually acquired its own being and cut itself off from its divine progenitors. It is this process which, at the beginning of the Bible, is presented in the story and the images of the 'Fall of Man'. The Fall is also called 'Adam's original sin', and is a fall into sin. The word 'sin'

Individualism is killing individuals.

actually is akin to 'sunder'. Keeping in mind the process of becoming independent it is describing a sundering from the parental Godhead.

This process can be compared with a nine-month pregnancy in the mother's womb, after which, from a physical, external point of view, the new being is separated from the being of the mother. The birth and the cutting of the umbilical cord are stages in the gradual process of one being becoming *two* separate, independent beings. We see here what a very complicated and slow process is involved. It is not something that happens in one single moment and which can be reduced to one or another particular aspect.

After the Flood 'Religion' Begins

Is it possible to be more precise with regard to the actual moment *when* the growth of human independence reached a certain finality? The answer given to this by Rudolf Steiner's spiritual science is that the actual religious element — the endeavour once again to form a link with the sphere of the gods — is a specific phenomenon of the *post-Atlantean epoch*, i.e. the era after the Flood.

This era is preceded by the *Atlantean epoch* — which we find described by Plato and in various myths — during which humanity inhabited the geographical area now covered by the Atlantic Ocean. In ancient times a continent existed there from which came forth the whole of 'post-Atlantean' civilization.

In those times the air was impregnated with water to a far greater extent than it is today. The so-called 'Flood' occurred because the air was increasingly cleansed of its water content. Through this tremendous precipitation of water over long periods of time whole regions became totally flooded. This cleansing of the air, of the earth 'atmosphere' of its water, occasioned what is described in every legend as 'the Flood'.

In the Bible this event is also expressed in the fact that at that point—because the air contained much less water than before—a phenomenon of physics became possible for the very first time: the appearance of the *rainbow*. Noah is promised that a flood, a water catastrophe such as that, will never happen again, because it *cannot* happen again: the air now contained so little water that a second 'Flood' was not possible.

Therefore Jehovah can tell Noah that this token of the rainbow is given to him as a covenant of peace. And up till today the rainbow appears as a solemn token of peace between the Godhead and humankind.

However, through the fact of the atmosphere now holding less water, something else became possible, namely, the distinct clarity and sharpness of outline of *sense perception*. Because everything had previously been enshrouded in waterlogged air, the objects perceived did not have clear outlines. The customary clarity of our sense perception was possible only when the air and water conditions became, in the course of ages, as they still are basically today.

Alongside and parallel with this physical phenomenon of the appearance of clear, sharply-defined sense perception, human beings began to *perceive themselves* as physical, material beings, experiencing themselves more and more distinctly as separate from the Godhead. Thanks to the ever-increasing clarity of sense perception the human being began to feel more and more at home in the physical world. At the beginning of the post-Atlantean epoch, the post-Flood era, human beings began to feel at the same time 'homesick' and became more and more *religiously* inclined. They sought to reconnect themselves to the sphere of the gods, and wanted to return to a lost 'Paradise'.

If we consider the post-Atlantean cultures—the Indian, the Persian, the Egypto-Chaldean and then the Graeco-

Latin culture, we notice that these post-Atlantean epochs of culture also represent in the most literal sense of the word the stages of the religious evolution of humankind. These cultures arose in order to enable the people of each epoch to seek the lost heavenly Paradise in their own way.

The 'lost Word of God', i.e. the initially existing direct experience of the supersensible element in all things, had to be sought for more and more out of the depths of human longing. The human being felt he had been thrown out of his original homeland so that he could seek for it and find it again. Especially in the fundamental religious mood of the ancient Indian culture we can feel the longing to find the way back to the original home of the spirit, to primeval Paradise.

'Expulsion from Paradise' and the Twilight of the Gods

In those times each human being was still endowed with what Rudolf Steiner calls 'atavistic clairvoyance': a God-given faculty of directly perceiving the supersensible element, the 'spiritual Word' in all things. This atavistic clairvoyance had in fact to disappear in the course of the post-Atlantean epoch. This gave human beings the chance to revoke the separation through their own initiative.

The New Testament parable of the Prodigal Son is a portrayal of this evolutionary mystery. The younger son, i.e. the later peoples of the post-Flood era, leaves his father's house in order to become independent. Out of the freedom and independence he has acquired—i.e. thanks to the inner transformation that has happened in consequence—the younger son returns to his father's house because he will now be able to experience a totally new communion with his heavenly father which he himself, in freedom, has worked to bring about.

What is presented in this parable, as a parable of the

whole of human evolution, is described in a modern form in, for instance, Rudolf Steiner's *Occult Science*. A description is there given of how evolution took the direction of wiping out step by step the ancient atavistic and instinctive clairvoyance. This evolutionary process, in which every trace of an ability to perceive the supersensible world was gradually lost, is of course a very complicated one. Not only a communication with spiritual beings died out but, later on, also the connection with the elemental spirits of nature.

The Baldur myth of German mythology is a beautiful description of the death of the capacity to live in communion with the light-filled nature spirits. Seen in his spiritual reality Baldur is the shining elemental spirituality of nature. The Germanic peoples of ancient times could really perceive the gnomes, the undines, the sylphs and the salamanders. These were all very close to them and absolutely real.

The myth tells us — and this again is an aspect of the Fall, of the 'twilight of the gods', of the necessity for humankind to separate from the spiritual/supersensible realm — that the day came when Baldur was killed. Humanity lost the ability to perceive the light-filled world of the elemental nature spirits. And where did Baldur disappear to? Down to the darkness of Hel! Dark Hel (English: hell) is nature devoid of spirit, as perceived by the materialistic human being of today.

Compared to the light-filled spiritual form nature had in the reign of Baldur the world as we perceive it today would be for the ancient Anglo-Saxon peoples a veritable world of total darkness, a dark 'Hel', comparable to 'hell'. An Anglo-Saxon who still had memories of being once upon a time with Baldur in a paradise of light knew that a world in which Baldur had died would be bound to be gloomy and sorrowful.

The fact that we nowadays do not experience the world as dark is because we no longer have a memory of the light-filled spiritual form of nature. We have no means of comparison any longer, and nowadays we think the world is bright enough in the daytime, and that it has always been experienced in this way.

The central meaning of the Fall, the reason for the separation from the spiritual realm through becoming more and more deeply entangled in the world of matter, is *human individualization*. In the beginning humankind was all one being. 'Adam' does not mean one single person but a unified primeval humanity. To begin with there was one being of a 'group soul' nature in which there was as yet no experience of an individual ego. The meaning of subsequent evolution was that through a more and more extreme connection with matter a more and more pronounced individualization of humankind could arise. Matter is the principle of separation, of the division into single beings.

The final result of this process of individualization is our present condition in which each human being literally has the ability to experience him or herself as a separate independent, autonomous ego. We feel and experience ourselves as a unity enclosed within ourselves. We can think for ourselves and decide what our actions shall be and carry them out by virtue of our own individual insight.

If one were to ask further what the significance of this individualization is, one cannot give a theoretical or abstract answer any more. For something which is archetypally good, something which has the absolutely self-evident and blessed nature of the ego as inner spiritual autonomy, cannot be established on the basis of anything else — whether of a lower or higher nature. A human being who really understands himself knows from his own experience that ego-nature represents the highest rank and stage of the human condition.

He experiences it with direct 'evidence' as archetypal goodness, archetypal truth and archetypal beauty, and he is filled with gratitude for this universal ideal of evolution. He can do no other than approve wholeheartedly that it is granted to him to experience himself as an individual, free spiritual being. There is nothing further to 'prove'. Where this experience is not sufficiently present, proof is basically of very little help. For every proof is really only of value when it has been preceded by the experience of the reality to be proved.

For example you cannot prove that trees really exist. Nobody has ever proved that trees exist. Either they are experienced in their reality – and then one does not need theoretical proof – or we are dealing with a person who has never experienced trees (so how can one prove to him theoretically that they exist?). They do not exist for him because he has never experienced them. It is the same with the arising of individuality, with a real experience of ego nature. It has to be experienced, not proved. Each person needs to demonstrate it, not prove it.

Religion is a Returning Home – but in a Forward Direction

Just as the first phase of human evolution has separated human beings from one another and from their common heavenly home, the second half of evolution will be such that we human beings, by means of exercising our ego nature and making it more and more real, will strive towards a reconnection, which is what *religion* is – a reconnection with all spiritual beings, all human beings and all creatures. This is happening at present to the extent that individual freedom has been achieved.

This reconnection, however, must not take place through a cancelling out of evolution and a return to the primal condition. Human individuality has not arisen and become reality in order to be annulled! A future communion with the whole of the heavenly, human and natural realms reached by way of humanity's religious paths will be quite different from the communion which was there in the beginning.

The character of oneness in the beginning was a kind of uniformity without structure and variety. The communion accomplished at the end will possess quite a different quality. When all human beings become part of one another again through ever further stages of spiritualization, thereby regaining the accompanying communion with the spiritual Hierarchies and all the creatures of nature, this will not extinguish each human being's individuality but, quite on the contrary, will bring it to final completion.

The unique ego-nature of each human being can no longer be annulled. This reconnection with the spiritual cosmos and with all the other human beings will be achieved by means of religion. This practice of religion achieves at one and the same time the genuine perfecting of the individuality. Just because this building of the spiritual organism of humanity—which in Christian tradition is called the 'spiritual body of Christ'—can only happen through the exercise of individual freedom and love, through the unfolding and application of all the *individual* forces of the ego, it will bring about gradual perfection and not the extinction of the individuality. In the course of this process, all the forces potentially inherent in each human being in an individual and unique way will be called into life and made manifest. In the process of that archetypal polarity of evolution occurring in a series of time spans, where the initial one-sidedness of the beginning—the one-ness without individuality—changed to the second one-sidedness—the splitting into separate individuals, involving the loss of a truly spiritual communion—there arises the further task of evolution. The third phase will see the aspiration to achieve a synthesis of both these. Communion and individuality shall no longer be experienced one without the other, or actually in opposition to one another, as mutually exclusive. Individuality shall now gradually attain perfection by mirroring within itself, and experiencing and helping with a love-filled heart, all other beings, human and otherwise. The mirroring of all of humanity in the individual is the final perfection of the individual himself. On the other hand our belonging together needs to become more and more an experience of a communion that owes its ever-increasing richness and variety to the unique and special contribution of each individual. Communion will therefore only blossom with the affirmation and willing support of each individual. Communion can only be experienced as a common treasure in its valuable multiplicity and its overflowing abundance when each single member brings something different from everyone else to the general welfare of all.

The development of *religion* must also be seen from this evolutionary perspective. We really understand religion only when we grasp that the aspiration to reconnect with the spiritual realm is the whole meaning and purpose of the religious development of every single human being. The single religions are, each one, different aspects of this human evolution. It is important to start by understanding this common element in evolution, for only then can we understand the special contributions of each of the different religions.

So religion begins where the human being starts to experience himself as having been thrown out. Religion arises where the human being—becoming conscious of his loneliness—begins to reconnect himself with the spiritual world in his search for the kingdom of God.

The Methodical Perspective of Evolution

If we apply the systematic centering of the perspective of *evolution* to the religions we suddenly make an astonishing yet profoundly liberating discovery. Where evolution is taken seriously we cannot consider any religion as either good or evil in an absolute sense. Each religion is good if it represents a promoting of the good of humanity according to the *spirit of the times*. Everything hindering the current evolutionary stage of humanity is evil.

If we understand the first half of evolution as predominantly the work of divine Grace in paving the way for human freedom, we can say: the religions *before* the turning-point of time are much more the work of the Godhead than of human beings. In this sense all the religions before Christ were 'good'. They were willed by the gods, divinely inspired, and the hand of God guided them. The founders of the religions received *from the Godhead* what was good and right for their particular time, both for their own people and for humankind.

If we now come to speak of the *religions* of humankind in the plural we can understand this multiplicity on the basis of the essential division of humankind already discussed, and which has to come to an end at the ultimate divisibility, the indivisible 'atom' of the individual, the ego. This process of division and differentiation has to begin with a division into larger groups.

The first large differentiation among humankind occurred in the remote past by means of the *separation of the sexes*, whereby there arose two different ways of being fundamentally human. This very first division was carried further through the development of different races, and later on different cultures. The races manifest fundamentally different bodily characteristics. On the basis of these differences in the bodily constitution there appeared, especially in post-Atlantean times, different soul characteristics among the various nationalities. The Indian, Persian, Egypto-Chaldean and Graeco-Roman epochs are *cultural stages* as distinct from the *natural stages* of racial manifestations.

Atlantean times were sustained by bodily features. In post-Atlantean times psychological/cultural characteristics were prominent, and these were expressed by the various peoples in their religious mythologies.

So the pre-Christian religions arose parallel with the arising of the different peoples. Fundamentally they are all therefore *national religions*. In the perspective of reincarnation each human being incarnates into each of these various national qualities—and therefore also into their various religious practices. Each human individuality evolves further and further by passing from one religion to another. Therefore we can regard the religions before Christ—before the turning-point of time—as stages of the past evolution of each human being.

The significance of the 'turning-point' is that the substance of what previously manifested in the various nations and religions one after the other or one alongside another (i.e. in the separate expression of the qualities of each one, which inevitably involved demarcations and mutual exclusiveness) had to be brought to a universal synthesis and harmonization in each human being and experienced as the outcome of freedom in each one. To make *this* possible and to set it in train was the meaning and purpose of the entry of the 'Son', of the Being of Love, into Earth evolution.

I should like to put it this way. The rise and growth of the various peoples and religions—together with their mythologies—before the turning-point of time is, to start with, less the work of human freedom than of divine guidance and the Grace of God. However, the purpose of this divine guidance is that it enables each human being, in the age of freedom, to acquire voluntarily and in an individual way—bringing them together and making them his own—all the different *human dimensions* actively brought about one after another by God and initially divided among the various peoples.

From Religions to the Human Being as Religion

To the extent that after the turning-point of time a conscious, freely developed synthesis of all religious qualities, all the experiences resulting from the reconnection of human beings with the realm of the heavens, are felt to be increasingly real, one can no longer speak of 'religions' in the plural. We find we gradually become entitled to speak simply of 'religion'. In this sense we can say that every human being is individually called upon to realize *in himself*, in the course of his future evolution, the synthesis of all the religions. As an individual person, each man or woman is called upon to bring to realization in themselves the harmony and the perfection of all the possible ways of relating to God.

The *human being himself* has to become the religion which is gradually growing in substance as it comes to realization on earth. The perfect religion — the religion of all religions — is the perfected human being, the final goal of Earth evolution. In the human world there is nothing more 'religious' than man himself.

This concept of religions in the plural which we have, out of freedom, to make into 'religion' in the singular is at one and the same time the true 'Christian' concept of religion. It is also the concept of the 'fullness of time' or the 'turning-point of time'.

It was at the central point of time that the Sun Being, the central spiritual being of our solar system, through whose very deed the first half of evolution was brought to fulfilment and the second half opened up, departed from the sun to unite himself with all the forces of the earth and of humankind — he who has nothing incomplete or exclusive within himself but embraces the whole gamut of evolutionary impulses pertaining to the earth and to man.

Because of this event each human being was granted the ability to overcome everything leading to divisiveness, everything which still divides and separates one human being from another. Every 'sectarian religion' should be overcome in the sense that in each one-sided religious impulse there is the desire to merge in the one universal religion, which is only to be found, however, in the perfected wholeness of the *human being himself.*

Therefore, in the course of time, everyone will face the task of forming his relationship to the heavenly realm in such a way that it does not continue to give one particular aspect precedence over others but that a kind of synthesis of religions is aimed for which would totally exclude the possibility of several 'religions' existing side by side or actually even working against one another.

This goal seems on the face of it to contradict the fact that Christianity, too, has, during the last two thousand years, been taking on the form of one religion among and along-side — and often enough *against* — other religions. However, this fact has itself to be understood from the point of view of evolutionary necessity.

The Change of Direction is Not the End but Only the Beginning

The Sun Being, with his universal and harmonizing influence, did not enter the earth and humankind in order to bring about, entirely by himself with the exclusion of the co-operation of human freedom, the synthesis of the religious life with all human striving. On the contrary, he came to create the actual *necessary conditions* to enable each human being to realize the one universal religion in himself. His love comes to expression in the evolutionary *ability* he gives to each one of us.

These essential conditions are not a matter of mere teaching or theory. The essence of the Christ event and Christ's ministry consists not in what he said but in what he *did* and what he is *continuing to do*. This stream of activity, which has been coming from the Being of Love for the past two thousand years, has gradually so transformed all the forces of the earth and of humankind that their inherent determinism no longer forbids but allows for the possibility of an inner experience of freedom.

This means that the essence of *past* 'Christianity' was the actual activity of Christ himself, and that *beginning in our time* the human being — thanks to Christ's activity — is acquiring the faculty to bring about the synthesis of all religions in his own being from out of his own freedom, even though this freedom is only in its first beginnings.

Before the turning-point of time the 'Father' God called forth the different 'religions' in the different peoples as evolutionary opportunities for the human race. The 'Son' God brought about the turning-point in time in that he created the actual conditions and the actual capacity in each human being — and he needed time for this process — so that each human being, in himself and in freedom, would be able to overcome every religious one-sidedness, each human one-sidedness.

The appearance of a truly modern spiritual science marks the actual beginning of a decisively new stage of the formation of religious life in humankind. This new stage does not consist of some new 'religion' being founded. It is inherent in the very nature of Christianity itself that the epoch of exclusiveness has to be left behind. What is new in our time is the opportunity for each human being to become *conscious in his thinking* of the synthesizing character of Christ's activity, which enables each human being to tackle his or her relation to religion as their own *free deed*.

Rudolf Steiner's most modern spiritual science allows for the first time for the possibility of striving for a *fully conscious* and *totally free* form of religious life — of relating to the divine/spiritual element of the cosmos — as the fulfilment of Christ's activity, as an actual experience of the Holy Spirit, which the Being of Love is willing at every moment to pour into each human being.

This Holy Spirit, which only the *religion of freedom* recognizes to be the religion of man, is nothing else but the Spirit of Christ himself, for the Being of Love can only desire and awaken the spirit of freedom in each human being. When a person brings the Spirit of Christ alive in himself he will experience the 'second coming' of Christ in the most actual sense, the reappearance of Christ in his own thinking and loving spirit.

One can also say: spiritual science as initiated by Rudolf Steiner is the start of the true *religion of the Holy Spirit*, of the healing, liberating spirit in each human being, the beginning of the religion of man and of humankind altogether, whereby the fourth, the 'supreme' respect Goethe speaks of in his *Wilhelm Meister*—self-respect—has to be consciously grasped and more and more intensely experienced as the evolutionary task of all future 'religion'.

The Religion of the Northern and the Southern Peoples

Rudolf Steiner speaks about the fact that in the epoch of religions, of the particularized and partial aspects of human communication with the heavenly realms which arose in the various peoples, one after another, we can distinguish two fundamental streams: a Northern and a Southern one. In the *Northern stream*, which especially concerns the Persian peoples, but also the Celtic-Germanic peoples, one of the fundamental forms of 'reconnecting' with the spiritual world was practised in that a human being was initiated into the far reaches of the cosmos by being led out into the macrocosm in a state of ecstasy.

The *Southern stream*, the basic Southern form of religion, which manifested especially in India, then in Egypt and later on in Greece, consisted in the endeavour to experience

the heavenly realm within man's own inner being. The
human being entered into his own inner nature by way of
mystical experience. This Southern initiation into the micro-
cosm of 'man' brought about quite different experiences
than the initiation into the macrocosm.

These two archetypal forms of humanity's religions —
experiencing the supersensible realm by expanding into the
far reaches of the macrocosm or by becoming absorbed in
the soul's inwardness — can be found in the greatest variations in all religions and also in all folk mythologies.

The synthesizing nature of Christ's activity can also be
seen with regard to this polarity. The two fundamental
pillars of experience bearing on the *incarnation* of the
Christ Being correspond to these two archetypal forms of
religion.

The process of contracting into human inner nature is
presented in the baptism in the Jordan and in the subsequent threefold 'temptation'. The threefold temptation of
Christ is the condensed experience of all Southern paths of
mysticism, of the absorption of the human being in the
depths of his own nature. This is where the entire force and
reality of *egoism* is experienced. This is where one realizes
that the religious task of all future paths of development
will consist in the overcoming of egoism.

After three years, the Christ as human being experiences
the second basic form of human religion in his *death and
resurrection*. He 'goes to the Father', expands into the
macrocosm and unites with all the forces which are active in
the earth.

The picture of Gethsemane shows the moment where *fear*
is experienced as the ever-recurring archetypal experience
of the Northern type of connection with the heavenly realm,
where the human being expands into the macrocosm.

The human being experienced fear because he was
threatened by the danger of losing himself and dissolving in
his efforts to unite with the infinite reaches of the cosmos.

He had to be afraid lest he should lack the strength to remain fully concentrated within himself, because his ego-nature was after all only just beginning to develop. The word 'ecstasy' expresses the fact that the human being had to lose his self-consciousness in those days in the expanses of the cosmos.

The polar opposite of this Northern experience of *fear* was the Southern experience of *shame*. In the course of concentrating himself within his inner being a human being experienced shame at the enormous amount of egoism and self-centredness each human being has to experience if he can see himself objectively.

Within his own being he perceives all that has brought him — in fact was bound to bring him — to the point of experiencing himself as the centre of the world. Ego-nature and individualization has only been possible because of the fact that each person had to learn to lay claim to all the forces of the world for himself — just as each child has to do so. Simply to become an individual person a child has to begin by being a real 'thorough-going egotist'. He has to demand for himself all the forces of the world and every other human being. Thus in concentrating in himself a human being learns what it means that he had to 'make use' of all the forces in the world and everybody else. He sees what he has deprived all the other beings of in order to claim it for himself.

The overcoming of shame consists in a human being realizing that this necessity of egoism is not a negative fault but a task for the second half of evolution, the task of inner purification. If one understands it in this way, the relationship to oneself does not stand in opposition to the relationship to everyone else. 'Self-love' need not be got rid of but has to be extended to include everybody else. This is the meaning of the Christian statement: 'Love your neighbour as yourself'. Each person who has become egoistic will now be able to overcome egoism in that he gives back to humanity, and engages for the benefit of everyone else, all those forces which he himself has initially received.

Initiation in the Mysteries as the Origin of Religions

These two basic manifestations of the pre-Christian religions point to a further decisive factor in the evolution of religions: the *Mysteries* of the ancient world. We cannot possibly underestimate the role the Mystery Schools played in the general and also the religious evolution of humankind.

In the Mystery Centres there were initiates who anticipated 'before their time' future stages of human evolution. They trained pupils to be able to have communication with godlike beings, and these pupils were then capable of imparting to their people the will of the gods both as an evolutionary task and as religion.

Through regaining a connection with the spiritual world — through *initiation* — the leaders of humanity were able from out of a direct relation to the spiritual world to give their people the proper religious impulses. They learnt from the divine being guiding the specific task of the nation whose leadership was entrusted to their care. They passed this evolutionary task on to their people in the form of 'religion', i.e. in the form of religious practice. The true origin of the religions lies in the inspirations sent down from godlike beings to these initiates in the form of impulses for the development of the various peoples.

Thus for example the Zarathustra religion comes from the relationship of the individuality of Zarathustra to the spiritual world, especially to the spiritual Being of the Sun, with the mighty Sun Aura, as he called it, Ahura-Mazda. It was granted him to learn from the spiritual world which particular religious practice the Persian people were privileged to practice and to bequeath to humankind as a whole.

The role the initiates played in the Mystery Schools, in the

Mystery Centres, was a twofold one. On the one hand they initiated the few human beings who were capable in the days of the ancients of working on inner development in a way that led without harm to initiation. On the other hand it was the duty of these initiators to guide their peoples' task not only in a spiritual way but also politically and economically. They determined both the daily life and religious practice as expressed in the cult.

All the cultic practices, all the rites of the peoples, are actually a transference for the people as a whole—and in this sense turning them into something exoteric—of what was experienced esoterically in a real way in the schools of initiation. The cult of the various religions is a symbolic picture—meant for the whole nation—of the experiences undergone by the pupil along the path of initiation. In the religious enactment of the cult a presentation was given in picture form for the people as a whole of the experience undergone in initiation in a real, spiritual way.

The difference between *religion* and *mythology* consists in the following. Religion is the popular version of what happened in the Mysteries in the course of initiation, expressed more from the point of view of will activity and action, whereas mythologies represent a more cognitional and narrative interpretation of the same process of initiation. Thus in *ritus* and *mythos* the people as a whole were given a 'popularized' or exoteric version of esoteric initiation experiences. The simple people were educated by way of cultic rituals and mythological narratives. Mythologies and religions have been the great educators of the human race.

We find in the Gospels in the way in which Christ teaches and is active among humankind the last echo and at the same time a synthesis of both the narrative mythos and the active ritual.

To the people he always spoke in images, in parables which sum up the mythologies of all nations. To the few who showed a higher level of development he presented the esoteric side, where the moral consequences can be drawn for one's life and for one's deeds. To those people he explained in conceptual form the deeper meaning of all the parables, pointing to *his* initiation, death and resurrection, as a summing up of all the initiation experiences, of all the pre-Christian Mysteries, as a real synthesis of all the religions. The all-embracing religion is the whole of evolution itself as death and resurrection of every 'son of man'.

The essence of every religion is the endeavour to overcome death. The human being needs to 'refute' death in the sense that he needs to have the experience that he is more than what is manifested materially and, as a purely spiritual being, cannot be harmed by matter and will continue to exist without a physical component after death and the decay of his body.

This initiation in the Mysteries was always an anticipation of death as the victorious entry of the human spirit, after leaving his body, into the actual experience of the spiritual world.

Just as initiation was an anticipation of death, the religions were likewise, for the people, a popular imitation of the experience of initiation. In this sense religions are presentations, on the various levels of the different populations, of the manner in which, through initiation, a human being unites in his real being with the spiritual world. This gives him the experience of being himself a purely spiritual and eternal being. Matter is the place of his individualization, but his true being is untouched by the laws governing matter.

The essence of initiation as an overcoming of death, or the essence of religion as an overcoming of death—each of these is a reconnection with the spiritual realm through the overcoming of the laws of matter.

The mythologies present the same thing in a more narrative, pictorial form, without the recipient directly 'doing' anything—as in a ritual or religious service—except living inwardly in soul-stirring pictures. The content of the mythologies is therefore the same as the content of the corresponding religions, and the synthesis of both of them portrays the mystery of death leading to resurrection in a spiritual world.

All Religions Apply to Everybody

An important aspect of Rudolf Steiner's spiritual scientific view of religions is the difference made between the individuality of each single human being and the various religions each individual human being goes through and makes his own in the course of his development. Each religious dogmaticism can only be overcome if none of the religions is presented simply as true or as false. In the perspective of evolution all religions will be recognized as justified and necessary in their turn. Each one arose as an embodiment of the impulse of its time, and therefore as an essential transitory stage of the evolution of humankind. All the particular religions are acceptable to the extent they are directed towards the overcoming of every division through the embedding of their particular quality into a universal whole which is the evolutionary perspective of each single individuality.

The awareness of the actual progression of the ever-developing *human individuality* from 'religion' to 'religion' will overcome the other aspect of dogmatism, namely, the ever-recurring temptation to identify the human individuality with a single religion. By means of the fundamental evolutionary law of reincarnation all the particular religious practices — the various national religions — are partial aspects of the all-embracing religion which is the gradual growth to 'humanhood' of each human being. Because each person's initial experience of a step-by-step progression is ultimately turned into a living whole by the human being himself, there arises universal humanhood on the one side and ego-centred individuality on the other.

Everybody has at some time been a Hindu, a Hebrew, a Greek, a Persian. In this sense we may never identify the human individuality with some particular religion. The same applies with respect to the races and peoples. Nobody can be identified with any particular bodily or soul manifestation because in the course of his evolution each human being makes *each* bodily type and national culture his own.

Just as before the 'turning-point of time' each human being will have lived through all the religions one after another and one without the others, every human being now faces his own inner turning-point to be achieved ever and again anew as each one of us, out of our own individual freedom, tackles the task of harmonizing all the 'religions'.

The fact that after the turning-point we still have different and separate religions one beside another has to be seen in the light of what still needs to be overcome. The modern task of religious development for each individual who has, in the first place through the mutual exclusion of the different religions, experienced all the various religious manifestations, consists in no longer experiencing these religious forms in their separate existence but in that of a reconciliation one with another. In doing this each human being will experience *himself* as the embodiment of the synthesis of all religions.

The synthesizing of the religions is like an anamnesis. In the *memory* of what was experienced aeons ago a new *awareness* of all the religions comes about in the deepest *depths* of our soul—remembering is becoming a member!— and this enables an interweaving and harmonizing to take place.

We can say the same sort of thing about religions in the plural as we can say about the races. In the course of evolution each individual has been incarnated into each racial form, in order to have the specific experience afforded by each 'external form'. It is similar with the religions. The religions in the plural which, before a synthesis became possible were experienced one after the other by each human being, are also to be understood as an 'external form' in so far as they were, in their time, an external gift of the gods.

Each human being is an eternal individuality bearing within him the dynamic to breath his own life into the special and particular qualities he once manifested, one after the other, as the sheaths of the different religions, so that each one of them will lose its fragmentary nature. Thus the sheath-nature will be overcome to the extent that the particular exclusive character defining it as a sheath is overcome. Religions which were divine revelations and which, *before* the turning-point of time, supported and carried the human being have, *after* the turning-point, to be brought together in the human being's own heart. This is the actual meaning of the statement in the Gospels: Take up your bed and walk. You shall now yourself carry in freedom all those impulses which carried you in childhood.

Each human being is called upon to make the many religions into *one religion*. The essence of what manifested originally in successive stages as external form takes on *substance* when the *being of man* arises through the inwardizing and harmonizing of all the religions, in the kind of self-awareness and self-development that is never-ending.

Thus the religions — in the plural — were outer garments which each human individual wore one after the other. A turning of the times happens whenever a human being endeavours to change each religion from an outer garment into an inner reality within himself. He is doing this when he makes them into a unity, when he makes *himself* into their living unity. He brings the religions together by making them part of human nature, part of his own being, which becomes in this way a spiritual part of *one unified humanity*. Thus humanity itself becomes the synthesized religion of each human being.

2
EASTERN RELIGIONS BEFORE CHRIST

In the fourth lecture of the cycle on the St Mark's Gospel,* Rudolf Steiner describes the different manner in which the Buddha, Socrates and the Christ presented their teaching. In this description, which is a summary of the important impulses in humanity, we see how religions and the religious life evolve, in pre-Christian times, from the East to the West by way of Greece.

First we see the Buddha endeavouring to bring his teaching alive in his pupils. The goal of his teaching was to pass on to his pupils what he himself had learnt and achieved through his enlightenment. His aim as a teacher was that the wisdom he had as the Buddha should be poured into his pupils unchanged and unfalsified. A pupil is a good pupil of the Buddha if he accepts the Buddha's teaching of compassion and love so that his own inner being becomes more and more similar to his teacher, the Buddha. The goal has been achieved when his pupil has acquired the same soul content and the same inner conviction as the Buddha himself.

The way Socrates teaches is the exact opposite. He refrained on principle from passing on to a pupil, unchanged, anything that was part of himself — anything that had arisen as the result of his own individual effort. All he wanted was to stimulate a person to carry out his own activity. This was why he called his skill the skill of a midwife. The pupil was encouraged to produce his own thoughts and will impulses from out of his own being on his own initiative. Socrates did not want anything of himself to

---

*Rudolf Steiner, *The Gospel of St. Mark*, Anthroposophic Press/Rudolf Steiner Press, New York/London 1986.

be seen in his pupils. Nothing was intended to be accepted merely on his authority. Everything that went on in the pupil was expected to be experienced as his own, and produced by himself.

Once, and once only, did Socrates teach more in the manner of a Buddha; and once, and once only, did the Buddha teach more like a Socrates. Socrates taught like the Buddha shortly before his death, when he was about to enter the spiritual world. The Buddha taught his pupil, Sona, on one occasion in a discursive dialogue, like Socrates did, to get him to see and understand something for himself.

We find in the Gospels a methodical and thoroughgoing synthesis of these two ways of dealing with pupils, when the Christ, acting like a Buddha, teaches the common people in pictures and parables. These pictures work in the listeners even without their conscious and independent co-operation. With the pupils who were prepared for it, namely, the apostles, the Christ behaves like a Socrates. In their case he endeavours, by discussing an interpretation of the parables, to appeal to and stimulate their discursive and active thinking, so that each one of them could see the connections through his own insight.

The Buddha, Socrates and the Christ

If we visualize this threefold approach to people — the way of the Buddha, Socrates and the Christ — we see an epitome of the entire meaning of evolution.

The way the Buddha taught is typical of religious practice in the eastern religions before Christ. In a certain sense we see in Socrates an anticipation of the fundamental character of human communication and also the practice of religious life as it developed in the time after the coming of the Christ. In the way the Christ taught we have a synthesis of both these ways.

The Christ affirms the justification of the old way by pursuing a Buddha approach with the common people. By linking up with the past he creates as many transitions as he can. People are always in need of this, because evolution can only proceed through a *gradual* transformation of the old into the new. Therefore with the common people the Christ is like a Buddha, turning to what is old and prior to the age of the ego as to the substance which has to be transformed. This approach summarizes all the eastern religions and confirms their preparatory character.

On the other hand where the Christ proceeds with his intimate pupils like a Socrates, we see in his way of working an anticipation of all future evolution. In the second half of evolution, in the time after the coming of the Christ, each human being is called upon to activate his thinking more and more in an individual and independent way so as to gain a better and better comprehension of the phenomena of evolution, and to act out of his own understanding.

At the same time this points out the basic character all religions possessed before the Christ. That was an era of human evolution which bore a preparatory character. That was the time in which successive religions manifested different qualities in human beings due to people being embedded within their particular people, and through this in the keeping of God.

If we see this against the background of the threefold membering of the human being into body, soul and spirit, we can say: Atlantean evolution brought forth the basic *bodily* manifestations through the different races, whereas post-Atlantean folk religions represent the basic stages of *soul* development. In this period of time an individual human being was not yet able to experience, as an ego-*spirit*, as a distinctly independent individuality, any real autonomy within his group, his folk or his religion. Initially a human being was part of and supported by the group, similarly to the way a child lives in the care of his parents.

The Bhagavadgita and the Epistles of Paul: a Conclusion and a New Beginning

There is a small cycle of lectures by Rudolf Steiner called *The Bhagavad-Gita and the Epistles of Paul** in which he points out that the spirituality that manifests in the *Bhagavadgita* exhibits a perfection not only of content but also of form. We could give a better picture of this if it were possible for us to experience the original meaning of the expressions in the Sanskrit language.

In contrast to this we find in the Paul epistles so much that seems in the first place to be entirely 'human', and which, in comparison to the *Bhagavadgita*, we must describe as being much less perfect. Both from the point of view of form as well as content Paul appears to be less perfect than the *Bhagavadgita*.

With regard to Christian texts, therefore, the objection often comes from eastern sources that the utterances of Paul are very imperfect. They say that he often becomes so personal! He allows his passionate human nature to show through, time and again, in his epistles. How can this 'Christian' element be considered more perfect compared to the contents of a text such as the *Bhagavadgita?* This is divinely inspired through and through, but where is divine perfection in Paul?

If we approach this puzzling question in a spiritual-scientific way we learn from another direction about the meaning of evolution and its various different stages.

There is no question of it: where its content and form are concerned the perfection of the *Bhagavadgita* as pearls of eastern religion cannot be surpassed. Neither the depths of its contents nor the perfection of its language and form have ever been surpassed. But the very thing that is important is that we have to do with something which, in its own way,

---

* Anthroposophic Press, New York 1971.

cannot be improved upon. We have to do with a conclusion, with something that is so accomplished that it has reached an end. The evolution of religion could not possibly have progressed any further in this direction.

Whenever a final conclusion and an ultimate accomplishment has been achieved in any particular direction, however, evolution has to begin again *from another side* if it is not to come to a complete standstill.

The sacred writings of the eastern religions owe the perfection of their contents and their artistic beauty to the fact that in an actual sense they were not human creations but were given to humanity as revelations from the divine-spiritual world. This is in fact the significant difference between pre-Christian religions and religion after the turning-point of time.

Before Christ, the fundamental character of religious life consisted in the fact that in the era of humanity's childhood the Godhead took the leading role. The primeval wisdom which came about in pre-Christian religions by way of divine inspiration and instinctive clairvoyance had the character of godlike perfection. Human beings still possessed the ability to receive not human but divine thoughts from the Godhead itself.

In this respect, too, the turning-point of time brought about a reversal in the direction of evolution. Divine revelation gradually ceased to play an exclusive role. Little by little it made way for human activity springing in freedom. Human beings have gradually to take a part in creation. The first stages of this are bound to be modest and very imperfect, but the further stages are destined in the course of time to become more and more perfect.

Ancient clairvoyance disappeared to the extent that the Godhead gradually withdrew. The gods no longer intend that human beings shall be filled with divine revelation except through people's own striving. They want to awaken in human beings the faculty of making concrete use of the inner creative force of their own spirit, out of the whole gamut of what has been put at their free disposal, and in grateful awareness of the workings of Grace. By now human beings should be paying more and more attention to the cultivation of what they can themselves produce in a Socratean way out of their own freedom. The purpose of divine Grace is human freedom. The whole achievement of Grace is the creating of the capacity for freedom.

Blessed with Freedom: to Bless in Freedom

If a blessing, a gesture of Grace, were not meant to find its fulfilment in human freedom it would feel to a person, in his inner being, like a 'disgrace'. A person who understands Grace as the opposite of freedom, as a denial of it, totally misunderstands Grace. Someone who does not discover his freedom to be in actual fact the taking of full responsibility for his evolution makes the whole working of Grace null and void.

A human being carries out the creative will of the God-head only if he comes to meet the working of Grace and divine Love by exercising his own freedom. The Divine Beings have no intention of withholding from human beings the best thing they themselves have, namely, being creative. They want to impart this to human beings in the course of their evolution.

Where a human being becomes a fellow-creator, Grace does not become superfluous. Critics of Rudolf Steiner say that the emphasis he puts on human freedom is the equivalent of annulling Grace, and that his 'self-redemption' stands in opposition to redemption by Grace. This is a misunderstanding. An act of Grace which renders freedom possible is much more demanding than one which does not want freedom to come about and therefore compensates for its loss. When human beings begin to be fellow-creators,

Grace has considerably more to do than in the phase of their childhood when only the Godhead was active. The daily maintenance of all the preconditions for freedom is far more complicated and all-powerful than the administration of a world where there is no freedom.

Where freedom comes about, divine Grace acquires the additional task of making good all the damage and wrong-doing perpetrated by human beings in the initial stages of their freedom. Today they have only just begun to exercise freedom; and, to start with, this is more a freedom of egoism and of arbitrariness than a freedom of love. Every day divine Grace has to set to rights and re-establish order amidst the chaos that human beings are causing at the moment. It has become possible and necessary for the working of Grace to extend to greater heights and reach to further depths just because human freedom is being added to evolution.

Therefore we can say: a comparison of the *Bhagavadgita* and the Epistles of Paul gives us an overall picture of the evolution of religions and of humanity's religious life. The *Bhagavadgita* comprises all pre-Christian religious life and brings it to a perfect conclusion. It brings to expression the kind of religion in which divine revelation and Grace played an almost exclusive role, and where freedom only made its very first tentative appearance.

It is the other way round in the Epistles of Paul; here we have a new beginning coming from quite another direction. In the religious development of humankind after the coming of the Christ what the Godhead does is no longer the only thing that is of importance. A deciding factor, now, is what human beings can add to this from out of their freedom. The tentative beginnings, the unpretentiousness, the actual clumsiness we see in Paul may be highly imperfect com-pared to ancient divine revelation, yet from the point of view of the dynamic of evolution it ushers in a further stage. It is new, and bears within it the seeds of the future.

Evolution could not proceed from where the *Bhagavadgita*

ends. Such perfection cannot be further increased. Evolution continues with Paul just because he gives us the first beginnings of something entirely new. It is this very imperfection and hesitancy which shows that it has many millennia of potential growth ahead of it.

And this new characteristic is that this very quality of ego-nature, the personal, individual factor, the element of liberation—all that has been achieved by way of individual insight—has now to help determine the further course of evolution.

'For God giveth not the spirit by measure unto him'

In St John's Gospel (John 3:34) there is a sentence that says literally: 'For he who feels the ego reveals even in his halting words the Word of God: for God giveth not the spirit by measure unto him.' For 'by measure' the Greek expression is ἐκ μετρου (*ek metrou*). This is usually translated as: 'For God gives the spirit without measure' or 'gives the spirit boundlessly'. Yet in Greek it does not say 'without measure' or 'boundlessly' but literally 'not with verse and metre'.

Rudolf Steiner gives an explanation of this verse—which has always remained a riddle to theologians—which I find very enlightening. The Cosmic Son, sent by the Father, comes to initiate human freedom. The realm of natural necessity provides the whole basis and the working material for human freedom. The purpose of natural necessity is freedom which, put in Christian terms, is expressed in the statement: 'the Father sends the Son'. This statement implies that human freedom is the meaning and purpose of natural necessity. Natural necessity calls for it.

In the verse just quoted it says: He whom the Father has sent speaks God's words as if 'babbling'. For 'speaks' the Greek says λαλει (*lalei*), and the German language has 'lallen' (akin to English 'lullaby') which describes a child learning to speak. Human beings are now beginning to let the words of God sound forth *out of themselves*, learning to speak *by themselves* in the way a small child does. Initially it is highly imperfect, like babbling, but it is the beginning of the unfolding of freedom. And now we can fully understand the other statement: He no longer gives forth the spirit in poetic form, with the god-inspired perfection of verse and metre.

The word *metros*, akin to *mantra*, stands for the poetic excellence of all ancient texts which were divinely inspired. The perfect form of the versification which fills us with such admiration in eastern writings, and many parts of the Old Testament, or in the *Iliad* and the *Odyssey*, was of divine origin. As poetry they are perfect just because they were given by the gods. Hence the word 'giveth'. This giving is the divine 'inspiration' that was customary in ancient times.

However, this is just what the Christ is bringing to an end. He does *not* give the spirit in the perfection of poetry, in the perfection of the language of God. On the contrary, he now begins to speak as a human being in a 'halting way' at first, very unassumingly. In this way he wants to give all human beings the courage to speak out of their own ego. In their deepest being everyone can do it, has the right, the desire and the *will* to do it. Every human being is called upon to give forth from himself words which describe the things of God, the concepts of all the things which, through human thinking, grasp and manifest the essence of things.

Key phrases of this kind in the Gospel of St John can be taken as statements of principle covering the entire character of evolution. We are being told that the basic nature of religion before the Christ consisted in the fact that the spiritual content of the world was given in the form of inspiration, in God-given language of unsurpassed beauty. This was expressed in the poetic perfection of its metre and verse. The prophecies of the Old Testament and the Psalms were also inspired in this divinely revealed perfection of poetic form.

But this has now to come to an end. A space has to be made for the new impulse, whereby a human being is no longer content to be merely a mouthpiece of the Godhead, a focus for revelation and the working of the divine element in the world. This is the case with every other object, but where human beings are concerned ego-activity has to be there *in addition*. Human beings are striving for spiritual independence, striving consciously to become responsible for themselves, in answer to the working of Grace and the whole of existing creation. They are called upon to become fellow-shapers of the whole of creation's destiny.

Transmigration of Souls or Reincarnation?

A further important aspect in the understanding of eastern religions before Christ is the question of *reincarnation* or *transmigration of souls*. It is constantly being asserted that a fundamental difference between Christianity and eastern religions lies in the fact that in the latter there has always been the idea that human beings do not only live once but come down to earth many times. This question is absolutely central to the understanding of the evolution of religions in humankind from another point of view also, namely, that in Rudolf Steiner's spiritual science a new stage of Christianity is being introduced in which a *new* awareness of reincarnation belongs to the very nature of Christianity.

Rudolf Steiner makes a point of distinguishing his approach to reincarnation and the way in which he understands repeated earth lives from the approach we find in Hinduism or Buddhism, for instance, or, in its last echoes, even in Plato.

This debate between what Rudolf Steiner says regarding reincarnation in the sense of western Christianity and the idea of reincarnation in the eastern religions is all-important for distinguishing religious life before and after the turning-point of time, because this aspect hinges directly on the character of this turning-point as a *totally new beginning*. Here we have to take our start from the important distinction between *transmigration of souls* —'metempsychosis' in Greek—and *reincarnation* in the actual sense.

In the eastern religions before Christ the conditions were not yet ripe to speak of *reincarnation* of the human spirit in the actual sense. It is solely a matter of *transmigration of souls*, of the passing of the human *soul* from one embodiment to another.

Rudolf Steiner regards a human being as having not only a body and soul, but as having body, soul and *spirit*. This threefold division of the human being—called trichotomy—was known especially to the initiates of the first Christian centuries. It was suppressed in traditional Christianity, not least because initially the human *spirit* was only spoken of in the form of a prophecy of what each human being, in the course of his development, had to bring forth in freedom. The statement that a human being *consists* of body, soul and spirit is misleading. It is only in the course of their evolution that human beings are *called upon* gradually, through working inwardly on themselves in freedom, to *add* more and more spiritual substance to their life of body and soul. Human beings are destined to *become* a spirit in a more and more real sense.

The distinction between soul and spirit can be traced back to the double νοῦς (nous) of Aristotle. The latter distinguishes between the 'passive' and the 'active' mind, or nous. All inner phenomena to which a human being relates passively or receptively represents a *soul* element. The human being as soul is supported by and swept along either by his bodily nature or by the social group, with its laws and customs, to which he belongs. As a soul he can only be part of a group and not as yet an individual. He is a sheep who has not yet become separate from the herd.

However, in the part of him where the human being becomes more and more inwardly active and creative in the Aristotelian sense, he becomes ever more strongly *spirit*. Soul is passive and shares a group nature; spirit is active and individual. This is the basis of the *enormous* difference between soul — and metempsychosis — and ego/spirit — and reincarnation.

Reincarnation is the evolutionary law of the *ego*, of the human *spirit*. It is the evolutionary law of the eternal, spiritual individuality. One can only speak of reincarnation in the actual sense when a genuine ego-nature is present which remains identical to itself through *self-awareness* and which passes independently and in freedom from one life to another by constructing for itself one body after another. *Migration of the soul* happens whenever a human being still feels himself to be a soul, i.e. is still embedded in group nature, as an integral part of communal life.

The Soul, the Ego and Ego-consciousness

Just because in pre-Christian times ego-nature — individuality as a conscious experience of the ego — was possible only in a very rudimentary way, we cannot speak of reincarnation of the human spirit. Therefore in eastern religions we find the fundamental assertion that the human *soul* does not disperse along with the body but continues to exist in the soul element of the cosmos as a coherent force structure of desires, urges, instincts and passions. This soul structure combines again later on with a new body in order to have new *soul* experiences on earth.

Even in the era prior to the turning-point of time each human being was an ego, an individual spiritual being. The meaning of our many incarnations, of the repetition of life experiences in the physical world, is to acquire more and more *ego-consciousness*. As long as an ego-being is too little aware of itself it is still only *potentially* an individual being (as Aristotle and medieval scholasticism would say). However, this potential for the spirit is just the factor we have described as *soul*.

Ego-consciousness has the same relation to the spiritual being of the ego, to the immortal core of the human being, as the reflection in a mirror has to the real object being reflected. An ego that does not know it is an ego cannot as yet behave or act as an ego, as it does not yet know itself. It would be like a human being who has inherited a wonderful legacy but as yet knows nothing about it. So we see that the distinction between ego and ego-consciousness is just as important as the distinction between soul and spirit.

The most important factor about a human person being able to experience himself as a free being is not only that he is a spiritual ego-being, an immortal individuality, but it is furthermore that he becomes conscious of the awakening of an awareness of what he is. If we talk of ego-development happening in the course of time, we are referring primarily to the fact of a person becoming conscious of his own ego, for not until we become aware of our own ego does what we call freedom become possible.

Thus we can say that 'immortality of the soul' and 'immortality of the spirit' by way of ego-consciousness are two totally different things. We could, if we wanted to, talk of the immortality of animals. The soul forces active in the body of an animal do not disappear and pass away when the body is laid aside and perishes. They continue to exist, and they are taken back into the animal's own group-soul, which the peoples of old called its *species*, meaning a supersensible *soul* reality (*anima*, soul, is the same word as animal). This soul substance goes through 'metempsychosis' in the building up of a new animal body.

The human being, too, in so far as he presents a picture of all the human soul forces, does not pass away after death.

This soul substance continues to exist, only ceasing from that moment to be united with the body. Therefore the question regarding reincarnation in the *Christian* sense is whether — thanks to the turning-point in evolution — it has become finally and conclusively possible for a human being to become conscious of his own ego, of his own self as a spiritual being, so that in the course of his bodily existence a person experiences himself not only as *soul*, borne and supported by the social nexus in which he is embedded, but as an *ego*, as a separate, independent spiritual individuality, and is active as such in the world.

The Son of God entered humankind in order gradually to transform the different religions of the soul into one consistent religion of the human spirit. *Ego-consciousness* is produced through the repeated union with the body, and this brings it about that human beings after death, in a body-free state, also experience themselves as spiritual beings enclosed in themselves. And it is just this aspect which is the essence of what we can truly call 'human immortality'.

Immortal is Not Something We are but Something We Can Become

The fact that after death all kinds of traces of a human being are 'still there' does not signify that a human being still exists *as a human being*, as an ego-conscious and individual spiritual being. Even when a plant 'dies' all the material parts are 'still there' and enter into other combinations. This implies, however, that initially a human being has acquired only as a future potential the possibility of *becoming* truly immortal.

Immortality after death is in itself a gradual and individual achievement of evolution. Immortal is not something we are but something we can *become*. Immortality is no absolute magnitude but has degrees of intensity. Becoming an ego and 'becoming immortal' are one and the same. What continues to exist in a human being after death can be neither greater than nor different from what was in him before he died. Through death nothing is added to a person's being, only his body is taken away.

This, however, means that a person can speak of reincarnation of the spiritual ego as the human spirit only *after* the coming of the Christ, and then only in a preliminary way at first, because a genuine experiencing of himself as an ego was not possible at all before then.

The more active a person's experience of himself is as an ego in life, and the more ego-activity there is in his behaviour, the stronger will be his ego-consciousness — immortality — after death. Each and every human being is destined to become more and more 'immortal', which means more and more independent and free. Less and less should he shift the responsibility for what he does onto others. Ego-consciousness will become stronger and stronger the more that people take upon themselves the individual responsibility for their own evolution and for the evolution of humankind and the earth. The spiritual entity of the ego is after all a matter of evolution.

The perfection and completion of a human being's 'immortality' will be achieved when the individual ego no longer experiences any difference between his own evolution and the evolution of all other beings. The fate of the whole of humanity and the whole of nature will have become his dearest and most personal concern.

The Trinity of the Godhead and the Human Trinity

In practically all religions — even pre-Christian ones — the Godhead is frequently understood to be a *Trinity*. From the point of view of a 'comparative study of religions' this fact could lead to our thinking of the turning-point as relative. Therefore we need, if only briefly, to look at the fundamental difference in the way the Trinity of the Godhead was understood before and after the coming of the Christ.

There is a Hindu Trinity of Brahman, Vishnu and Shiva. There is an Egyptian Trinity of Isis, Osiris and Horus. The important question here is: what does the human being experience with regard to the Trinity of the Godhead, and what does it enable him to *become*? The answer to this question shows us another basic difference in the way human beings experienced the Trinity of the Godhead before and after the incarnation of the Christ.

In my book *From Christianity to Christ* I have endeavoured to show that all the Trinities of the Godhead in the pre-Christian religions are to be understood, in the Christian sense, as a Trinity of the *workings of the Father*. Brahman, the Creator, Vishnu, the Preserver and Shiva, the Destroyer, all function in the sense of the paternal Grace of God in the era when the introduction of human freedom was still altogether in a preparatory stage.

The *Christian* Trinity is different in principle in the sense that the Son allows for and introduces a totally new dimension of evolution — the dimension of human freedom. In this sense the Son of God in the Christian sense must never be confused with any of the sons of pre-Christian Trinities.

Where the Trinity of the Godhead is concerned, it is not sufficient to testify to it in a theoretical, abstract way. We must enter more concretely into the experience and the actual development a human being goes through when he relates in a religious context with one or another god. The important thing is not what has been said about it in the way of theological theory, but what actually happens to a human being, and in a human being, through his relationship to it.

Where is the Buddha Now? What is he Saying and Doing Today?

In the same vein, we see for example in Rudolf Steiner's spiritual science that what the Buddha said and taught is of less importance than what the Buddha *did* for humankind, which is quite a different matter. Such aspects are not realized at all unless we pass from theory to reality. Then the other aspect also acquires importance: where is the Buddha *now* and what is he doing *now*? If we reckon with the fact that he himself was not an abstraction but a very real being who brought his series of incarnations to a conclusion in the sixth century BC, he must still be real and active, now, in the spiritual world.

If people were capable of hearing his inspiration *today* would they hear the same thing as the Buddha was saying two thousand five hundred years ago? Has the Buddha not gone through any further development? Seeing that humanity, thanks to the Buddha's teaching and activity, has *completely changed* during these millennia, and that totally new stages of evolution can and must be achieved in our time than were achieved before, should we not expect that the Buddha, in his infinite love for all people, has today something *quite different* to say, and to do, than in former times, even if people are not capable of hearing him, or they want to remain with what he said long ages ago, thus becoming *disloyal* to him as a living being?

The very fact that out of his spiritual research Rudolf Steiner raises questions of this kind and gives answers to them brings us to experience how tremendously moving his spiritual science is. He follows the actual living Buddha in his evolution right up to today, showing us how suitable and helpful for the course of evolution the Buddha's teaching and activity was in the sixth century BC, and how differently the same Buddha inspires and works today in the spirit of our times.

The living Buddha knows that human beings have changed just because they have followed the advice he gave them which was right for those times. This is why he has something quite different to say to human beings today than he said before. This shows once again what an important part a methodical study of the perspectives of evolution plays in Rudolf Steiner's spiritual science.

Krishna and the Overcoming of the Blood

Let us take the example of the Hindu divinity called Krishna. Regarding the question as to who Krishna is, there are various perspectives all according to whether you are looking at his way of working at the beginning of Indian religion—about the seventh, eighth millennium BC—or whether you are looking at the inspirations he brought much later on to Arjuna in the *Bhagavadgita* while acting as his charioteer. Again quite different things come to light when we ask who Krishna is and how he works today? Where is he to be found, and what does he say to people today?

In the *Mahabharata*, to which the *Bhagavadgita* belongs, we find something quite astonishing. Krishna is the very person who tells Arjuna he should not hesitate to bring death to his blood relatives. Many people who want to see only 'kind actions' in eastern religions overlook the fact that one of the fundamental demands in the *Bhagavadgita* is that Arjuna has to find the courage to break through blood relationship and liberate himself from it.

In the past, development was based on the forces of close blood bonds. This had to be overcome. The gift of ancient, *atavistic* clairvoyance came through blood relationship and in-breeding. The people experienced the working of the Godhead in and through their blood. But now the time is approaching—Krishna tells Arjuna—when blood-bound clairvoyance will have an untimely and retarding effect. If you want to prepare the future, he told him, you must overcome and kill off in yourself the binding nature of the blood. From now on you must no longer submit only to the natural drive in the blood. There shall no longer be marriages among blood relatives. Marriage outside the tribe has to replace in-breeding, to enable individual freedom, which is independent of the blood, to come about. Blood relationship shall gradually give way to relationships of choice.

With great clarity this evolutionary threshold is described in the mythologies and religions of all peoples! For example the story of the rape of the Sabine women in Roman history. And also in the Old Testament where there are a great many references to what it means not to marry into one's own people, one's own tribe, one's own blood, but to break out from the magical/godlike force of the blood through a mixing with foreign blood. In the Gospels, too, we find significant references to this mystery, e.g. in the first of Christ's miracles at Cana in Galilee.

The word 'Galilee' means a mixing of the blood, of the peoples. The significant characteristic of 'Galilee' was just this mixing of the blood. The Christ could be active only where there were people who had at least begun to overcome *blood relationship* carried by the blood. Among these people he could initiate the second half of evolution which will be carried by *relationships* of choice. Here again we have a significant aspect of the great turning-point in evolution: the transition from blood relationship, representing the working of the Godhead in human beings, to relationships of choice, representing the addition of human freedom. The religions before Christ were religions of the blood; religion after the coming of the Christ should be the religion of freedom of choice.

So we understand why Krishna says to Arjuna: Fight bravely, say yes to the change which must necessarily come about in the course of evolution, namely, that blood must

now rise up against related blood, that the same blood must
no longer cling together, because future evolution requires
that everything of a group nature, which exists only
through the fact that blood is the determining factor, shall
be overcome.

What is Krishna's real nature as a spiritual being?
According to Rudolf Steiner he is a partial revelation of the
Being who incarnated later on in the Mystery of Golgotha in
Jesus of Nazareth of whom St Luke's Gospel speaks. In
Krishna there appear to Arjuna forces that remained pure at
the Fall of Man. This is the part of the soul of humankind
which remained innocent, and which some of the first
Church Fathers called the *anima candida*, the immaculate
soul. These are the human forces of the 'Tree of Life' which
were held back in Paradise. Only the Tree of Knowledge
was sent down into the earthly stream of the Fall. A part of
these unfallen forces of the supersensible Logos, of the
cosmic Word in the human being, appears in the person of
Krishna.

The fact that in Krishna we have to do with a real manifestation of the cosmic Word is seen in a wonderful way in
the part of the *Bhagavadgita* where Krishna discloses his own
being — and this is one of the gems of Hinduism. We are told
that in Krishna the being of all things is revealed, meaning
the divine-creative principle. Because the divine-creative
principle brings forth the whole of creation, Krishna is the
cause of all things. The innermost spiritual core of all things
and the active cause of the whole of creation — this is
revealed to Arjuna through Krishna.

So we hear in the actual words of Krishna: 'I am the spirit
of growth and becoming, its beginning, its middle and its
end. Among beings I am always the noblest of all who have
ever existed. Among spiritual beings I am Vishnu, I am the
sun among the stars, the moon among the lights, among the
elements I am fire, among the mountains high Meru, among
the waters the great cosmic ocean, among rivers the Ganges,

among trees Menge Asvattha, in the true sense of the word I am the ruler of men and of all beings who have life, right to the serpent among serpents who is eternal and is itself the ground of existence'(*Bhagavadgita*, tenth canto).

And it says further: 'This cause of the world — it is fire, it is the sun, and also the moon; it is also this pure Brahma and this water and this greatest of creatures. All the moments, and the weeks, and the months and the years and the centuries and the millennia and the aeons have come forth from him, come forth from his shining personality, whom nobody can understand, not above, not below, not all around nor in the centre where we are standing . . .'

Krishna, the Buddha and German Idealism

What is revealed in this way in Krishna in its supersensible, spiritually-real form, Rudolf Steiner links up with a totally different cultural phenomenon appearing in humanity, namely, *German idealism*. German idealism also speaks of the absolute being, of the being which is in all things and which, as something creative, manifests in everything.

However, there is a vast difference between the pre-Christian character of the *Bhagavadgita* and German idealism which bears the character of the Christian era. These divine thoughts were revealed by Krishna to Arjuna without the exertion of human thinking. In the case of German idealism, however abstract this thinking may at first appear, human beings acquire these same thoughts by their own efforts, through applying the greatest and most profound forces of their ego and of thought. In fact it is merely a sign of one's own lesser development if one cannot oneself go through the most sincere and burning struggles to acquire knowledge, as did those German idealists. For these idealists are the very best witnesses to the power of the human mind and to the struggle for freedom and creativity of the human spirit.

In the sixth century before Christ, long after the creation of the *Bhagavadgita*, we see the appearance of the Buddha, who brings together in a kind of grand conclusion all the old religious teachings that existed in the East. He gathered together at the beginning of the Greek cultural epoch all the divine wisdom which was revealed in the Vedas, in the Vedanta. Buddha's task was to bequeath all this to future humanity, because the times were then past when such things could still arise. All that had been revealed in past millennia had to be preserved in humankind as a memory.

Therefore Buddha's actual contribution to the future of humankind does not consist any more in the contents of a revelation; its primary value is not its wisdom. The importance of the Buddha lies in his emphasis on practical *exercises*, on the path, the *eightfold path*. Thus the Buddha actually transforms the eastern Hindu religion, in which the emphasis in the past was more on the wisdom it contained, as the revelation of the divine element in the whole world and in man, into a path of training, into something moral.

This had to be so, for humankind increasingly lost the ability to receive divine revelation. Human beings became ever more distant and separate from spiritual realms. Therefore the Buddha transformed the conceptual character of his message and changed the wisdom into morality by means of which human beings aspire to revoke the Fall through the practice of religion. The Buddha teaches human beings the path of inner purification, the moral path on which to find their way back and reconnect themselves with the world of the spirit.

The Philosophy of the Vedanta and Greek Philosophy

In order to see a different aspect of the fundamental character of eastern religion before Christ we can compare the philosophy of the Vedanta with Greek philosophy. In the seventh lecture in the cycle on the Gospel of St Mark Rudolf Steiner contrasts these two phenomena, showing us that in the Vedanta philosophy we have, as he says, 'clairvoyantly-perceived concepts' as distinct from Greek philosophy, which in the last centuries before Christ changes into something quite new, in fact into concepts which human beings themselves shape through individual struggle and experience in an inner, discursive, logically thought-out way.

Rudolf Steiner realizes it is not easy for a person of modern times to imagine seeing concepts clairvoyantly. But we can try to do this by looking deeply into the transition to Greek philosophy, into Plato's *Dialogues*. There you will find numerous examples of the transition from divinely revealed concepts to concepts acquired by human beings by way of discursive and logical dialogue. If for example you look at the Dialogue 'Theatet' you will find the very two stages of evolution we have been talking about presented as two basic theses compared with one another.

One of the speakers thinks that concepts are percepts. That is the one fundamental thesis. The antithesis to this is that the percept is the opposite of thought. Plato is giving an objective presentation of the actual transition in evolution. Both speakers are 'right' in the sense that each one is presenting a faithful and genuine account of his *own inner experience.*

One of them is an older man who still has the old way of experiencing the inner wisdom and thought connections at the same time as the sense perception, as was customary in eastern cultures and religions. Ancient revelations always came about in this way. The other speaker is younger, and he does not present the opposite thesis because he is of the opposite 'opinion'—as though it were a matter of two different 'theories'—but because he is in fact *experiencing* the thoughts in quite a different way. Both of them are describing objectively how they themselves experience the mutual relationship of percept and concept.

One of them describes the way he receives percept and concept *in one*, so that he is unable to experience them as different from one another. In his case we can still speak of 'clairvoyantly perceived concepts'. For him the percept is at the same time concept and the concept is a direct spiritual perception. Both are received as though from outside, revealed by the gods and given to the human soul in the form of inspiration.

The other one is a person who is hardly capable of experiencing himself in this way any longer. In this sense he also says what is 'true'. He is one of the first people in whom the percept begins to be experienced quite differently from thoughts and thoughts quite differently from the percept. To him, the distinguishing characteristic of a percept is that it is given, that there is no activity involved on his part because percepts are simply there. Where the thought element is concerned the opposite applies; the chief characteristic of his experience, where the addition of concepts is concerned, is that they are *not* 'given', that he does not receive them just as passively. When he thinks, a human being has now to be active himself, or no concepts would be there.

This is how we can understand the difference between Vedanta philosophy and Greek philosophy. In the philosophy of the Vedanta we still have 'clairvoyantly perceived concepts'. This belongs to the fundamental character of the eastern religion before Christ. Even the element of conceptual thought is a direct activity of the Godhead in human beings! Not human beings but God himself, by means of inspiration and revelation, brings it about in human beings that concepts and the Logos content of the word arise and are perceived.

Greek philosophy is the opposite of this. Let us look particularly at the rubikon that was crossed in the transition

50   THE GREAT RELIGIONS

from Plato—who, as we mentioned, still possessed the last
echoes of this—to Aristotle, who very clearly introduces the
new element to humankind through his 'logic', through his
approach to knowledge and his ideas. In his case, too,
although his 'theory' was quite new, it was his own actual
experience.

Aristotle's approach was the beginning of a totally new
way of tackling the realm of thought, of concepts, of logic.
Human beings now begin to experience thinking as their
own activity, as their own creation. The producing of
thoughts and the connecting of one thought with another is
considered to be our own doing. The cosmic Logos becomes
human logic. The human being now has to experience
himself as the creator of his own concepts, and take over
moral responsibility for his thinking. He must not continue
to consider and to experience concepts as something
produced in him exclusively by God.

In the Greek philosophy of the final centuries before
Christ we see a distinct preparation for the turning-point of
time, for the sweeping new possibilities that became
possible for humankind through the Mystery of Golgotha.
The great turning-point of evolution is also the turning-
point in all religions, from each being just a portion to all of
them coming together as one universal, harmonized whole.
From the point of view of world wisdom, of the cosmic
Word, human beings achieved in Greece the transition from
the era of divine revelations to the era of human striving.
This happens when thinking is mastered by an individual,
creative handling of thoughts.

The Buddha and the Christ

The best way to understand the eastern religions before
Christ in their true significance is to consider the real
spiritual relation between the Buddha and the Christ. This

relationship can at the same time be regarded as the archetypal phenomenon of the relation between the Christ Being and the founders of the other religions.

One of the great merits of Rudolf Steiner's spiritual science is that it presents from ever new points of view in what sense the Sun Being—called the 'Christ' in the Christian West—has a unique place in the whole evolution of humankind. The central event of the incarnation of the Sun Being, of the Being of Love, is not one more special happening, one among many. It is the very synthesis, the harmonizing of all the partial aspects of a comprehensively universal whole. The relation between the Buddha and the Christ is similar to the relation between Zarathustra and the Christ, between Krishna and the Christ.

Rudolf Steiner's fundamental statement regarding the way the Buddha and the Christ relate is that the Buddha is the great *teacher* of compassion and love, whereas the Christ is the actual *Being* of Compassion and Love.

The Buddha is the one who awakens an awareness in humankind of how necessary it is to cultivate the forces of compassion and love. Just because the Buddha's mission, entrusted to him by the divine guidance of humankind, consisted of awakening through his teaching and influence a *consciousness* of the need for love and compassion, something else became necessary which lay outside his mission.

For it is not enough that human beings become *conscious* of how necessary love and compassion are. They must also have within them the *actual forces* of compassion and love and not only the teaching. Where do the forces, the actual forces, come from?

Who is the Being from whom the human being receives the actual forces that bring the *reality*—not only the theory, the cognitional awareness—but the living substance of active love and compassion? It is one thing to know what one ought to become and quite a different thing actually to be able to achieve it in reality. It is one thing to know that a stove is there for the purpose of heating the room, so you tell it to do so, and quite another thing to put wood in the stove so that it will actually happen. The Buddha's great task was to draw the attention of humankind to the fact that the 'Fall', the atomizing of humankind into separate individuals, had progressed so far that the forces of egoism had already brought them to the point where alienation from one another and opposition towards one another had reached an advanced stage. The Buddha drew the attention of human beings to the fact that the task of evolution was now to overcome egoism through compassion and love.

In the sixth century BC, shortly before the turning-point of time, the Buddha drew the attention of humankind to the fact of egoism and the lack of compassion and love. He pointed to the necessity of the intervention of divine guidance to send actual forces into humankind that are of an opposite nature.

Just as the driving forces of the Fall engendered egoism which divided people and set them one against another — real driving forces, not merely theory — the Buddha said that forces of the opposite kind had now to be produced for the regeneration of humankind, and these, again, cannot come only from human beings. The actual forces of love and compassion must be poured into human nature so that each person has the possibility to overcome egoism in him or herself.

Therefore the fundamental difference between the Buddha and the Christ consists in this: the Buddha is the great teacher of the need for compassion and love, and the Christ pours into humankind and into the whole earth the real and actual forces of Love, in answer to humanity's increasing awareness of this need. Thus Rudolf Steiner confirms that what we are told in eastern religion about the bodhisattvas who become buddha one after the other is true. The last one to become buddha was the bodhisattva born in the sixth century BC and who achieved illumination in his twenty-ninth year. That was his last earthly incarnation. His successor will not become buddha for another three thousand years.

The Twelve and the Thirteenth

In the spiritual world the company of twelve archetypal bodhisattvas are grouped around a thirteenth. They are like great missionaries bringing to humankind the teaching of the various essential impulses. Yet they are all grouped around a thirteenth being. This thirteenth being relates to them as the sun relates to the twelve signs of the zodiac. All the bodhisattvas bow to this thirteenth being and receive their mission from him. It is he who brings to humankind the real essence of the impulses, when the bodhisattvas, each in their turn, have made humankind aware of them.

Here we have the macrocosmic image of the twelve signs of the zodiac being 'visited' by the sun as the image of evolution as a whole. The twelve great bodhisattvas take over from one another and become buddha in turn. The Sun Being, called in the West the Christ, has the task of working further on what human awareness has recognized as necessary. He makes this possible for human freedom by means of shaping earthly evolutionary conditions accordingly.

This actual distinction between the Buddha and the Christ is also contained in the sacred scriptures of the religions. We need only take the scriptures seriously, just as they are. If we look at the original texts of Buddhism, that is, what the Buddha actually said six hundred years before Christ, we see that Buddha was always trying to *awaken an awareness* in his pupils. We find no mention of the Buddha ever stating that he was the actual cosmic force of love and compassion.

Statements which the Christ made and which are

contained in the Gospels, such as 'I am the Light of the world. I am the Resurrection and the Life . . .' do not occur in the writings of Buddhism with regard to the Buddha. Genuine sacred scriptures are always true; they state objectively what the mission of the respective being presented.

So we can now have a better understanding of the fact that Christianity had to struggle very hard to really comprehend the central Sun Being. The struggle to understand the difference between man and God goes back to the struggle to understand the difference between what a buddha has brought to humankind and what has come from the Christ Being. The being called the Christ brings to humankind a cosmic impulse in the widest sense.

The Eightfold Path – Then and Now

If we look at Rudolf Steiner's book *How to Know Higher Worlds*, we find among the important soul exercises the *eightfold path* of the Buddha. The question forces itself upon us: is all this not exactly the same as Buddha presents in Buddhism? Are these not exactly the same eight soul exercises? Throughout the book, superficially at least, there is hardly a reference to the Christ event. Does the perspective of evolution possibly play no part here?

To answer this question we must consider the following. As we have already mentioned, Buddha states requirements which are summarized in the eightfold path. These demands, however, require the development of actual forces. In the broadest sense these forces were brought to humankind by the Being of Love.

Let us take one and the same individuality who, thanks to reincarnation, does these eight exercises the first time five hundred years before the Christ and again in the twentieth century. Are they the same exercises both times? Yes and no. The drift of it is the same, but its execution and the inner experiences resulting from doing it are totally different. It is not so much what you do as *how* you do it! Before the coming of the Christ these exercises could hardly be done with the strength of the individual ego. But after the Christ this becomes the all-important factor.

It is beside the point whether a present-day human being doing these exercises calls himself a Buddhist or a Christian. The important thing is that these exercises are done in a *present-day manner*. What is important is what a person experiences whilst doing them, what *happens to him* and what he becomes as a result of doing them.

Where the Buddha *and* the Christ work together in human hearts—where a consciousness of Good and the power to achieve it meet—then the manner in which the human being approaches 1) right thinking; 2) right judgment; 3) right speaking; 4) right action; 5) finding the right vocation; 6) acquiring the right habits; 7) gathering the right life experience; 8) practising the right meditation, will be ever *new*. He will be at one and the same time a good Buddhist and a good Christian, but he will be neither of these unless he fulfils the present-day evolutionary task as a *free human being*.

3
THE ZARATHUSTRA STREAM AND THE BUDDHA STREAM

The post-Flood evolution of humankind as the evolution of religion in the actual sense brought it about that the first form of religion, seen primarily in the Indian culture, was a religion of longing for the spiritual world. In the seventh and eighth millennia BC human beings were still endowed with instinctive clairvoyance. Many people still had experiences that led them to the spirit. They had memories of Atlantean times—memories of a stage of human evolution when human beings were united with the spirit in a far more real way.

So we can say: the first form of the religion of humankind, which each human being alive today has been through, bore the fundamental character of mourning for the loss of a direct connection with the spiritual world. Religion was filled with the longing to find the way back to the primeval lap of the gods, to Paradise, humankind's original home.

Because in those times the human being was not yet able to appreciate his connection with earthly matter as a task of his future evolution, we can understand actually why the first form of religion could come to expression in no other way than through an aversion to the material world. The physical world was seen as the scene of the Fall and of man's contamination, in fact as maya, the source of all illusion.

It was not yet possible to see salvation as a call to human beings to take upon themselves the earthly task of transforming the world of matter. The redemption and salvation of humankind were seen as consisting of human beings detaching themselves from matter, leaving behind them the earthly world and returning to the spiritual world of the gods. The longing of the Indian people to return to the paradise of humankind's original home became the first form of religious life.

Zarathustra and the Earth as the Sphere of Action

The second post-Atlantean culture became something quite different, and here the archetypal Persian form of religious life was founded by the great initiate Zarathustra. The totally new factor introduced into humankind by Zarathustra was the overcoming of the aversion towards the physical world through human beings becoming conscious of the positive meaning in their union with matter. This connection was now seen as a task, as the task of human evolution altogether.

For the first time the earth was regarded, by Zarathustra, as a sphere of action essential to human evolution. Admittedly, the material forces were ascribed to the dark godhead Angria Mainu (Ahriman), as forces adverse to the good forces. The new factor in the Persian religion was that the confrontation with the forces of darkness and of evil was now seen to be a necessary and positive task of evolution. In the Zarathustra religion (Zoroastrianism) human beings begin to accept the meaning of the earth.

Already in the fourth or fifth millennium BC Zarathustra could proclaim the mighty prophecy which has accompanied the whole of the post-Atlantean Mystery culture ever since, namely, that the spiritual Being of the sun, whom he called the great spiritual Aura, 'Ahura-Mazda' (Ormuzd) was already in those times drawing closer and closer to the earth with the purpose of gradually leaving the body of the sun to unite himself with the whole spectrum of the earth's forces in such a way that the earth would become his body.

Therefore Zarathustra saw it as the task of religion to worship this Sun Being and to accompany him on his way to the earth. This is how we can understand how Zarathustra could take such a positive attitude to the mission of the earth.

When we survey these two fundamental forms of religion, the ancient Indian, the first post-Atlantean religion, and the ancient Persian, the second post-Atlantean one, then basically speaking we have the two archetypal forms of all pre-Christian religion. The first one bears a more eastern character; human beings do not yet have the ability to appreciate the confrontation with the earth, and with the suffering bound up with it, as a positive task of evolution. The second one turns for the first time, through Zarathustra, in the direction of the task to be fulfilled on earth.

We have already indicated that in pre-Christian times the Zarathustrian form of religion could not yet be the decisive one. What predominated to start with in all the pre-Christian eastern religions was humanity's aversion to matter and the longing to be released from the evil of reincarnation. This was still the case with the Buddha shortly before the coming of the Christ. He, too, saw the task of inner purification as consisting in human beings coming to the point of no longer having the need to unite with matter. They are freed from the wheel of births. The thirst for existence, the longing to unite with matter is overcome and extinguished.

Zarathustra, however, pointed to the decision of the Sun Being to incarnate, and to his setting out on his way to the earth in order to *remain* incarnated in the earth for the whole second half of evolution so as to be with human beings and to make possible their whole evolution *on earth*.

The Two Trees of Paradise

These two archetypal forms of humanity's religious life are presented in the first book of Moses in the image of the *two trees of Paradise*.

One portion of the initial forces of humankind are allowed to descend in the stream of the Fall, presented in the image of the Tree of Knowledge. Other forces of the primeval soul of humankind are kept back in the spiritual world in a state of heavenly innocence. These forces are represented by the Tree of Life.

These two trees refer to the two parts of the substance of humankind which, in the course of post-Atlantean evolution, call forth the two fundamental forms of religion.

The Buddha stream is inspired through its deep connection with the forces that have kept their heavenly innocence. This is why, in eastern religions, we always find the aspiration to find the way back to the forces of the Tree of Life, to the heavenly forces of innocence.

On the other hand we have in Zarathustra the individuality who, after having first incarnated in Persia and initiated the Persian religion, continues to remain connected with the stream of the Tree of Knowledge, and who was the model for every further version of the second form of religion that loves the earth.

At the turning-point of time there comes about the reuniting of humankind's two religious streams. The two trees of Paradise become one again. The religion of the longing for the spirit appears concentrated in the Jesus as described in the Gospel of Luke. The religion of the love for the earth takes on substance in the Jesus of Matthew's Gospel. In the twelfth year of life these two become one.

The forces of the Tree of Knowledge are all the practical experience which, thanks to the Fall, human beings acquire in the course of reincarnating on earth. It is here that a human being learns, as his individualization and independence increases, to be able to distinguish through his own initiative between Good and Evil. He becomes more and more free and morally accountable.

The other religious stream is the veneration of the forces in human nature which have nothing to do with the Fall.

Throughout humankind, even today, there are still echoes of an awareness of these forces of innocence wherever people speak of the higher, true human ego. These forces appear on earth, for the first time, concentrated in the Jesus described in the St Luke Gospel and in the nineteenth Sura of the Koran.

These two streams—the experience of earthly Fall and of heavenly Grace—were diametrically opposed to one another, and right at the beginning they could not be borne by one and the same earthly individual. The human vehicle had first of all to be transformed on earth on each side in such a way that it would later become possible for them to unite.

The evolution of religion in humankind prior to the coming of the Christ is the unfolding of these two streams and the relation humanity forms, through its various peoples and cultures, with these two streams of forces that represent heaven and earth.

So we have to look out for this archetypal polarity of humanity's religious streams in post-Atlantean times. On the one side is the Zarathustra stream, concentrated in the focal point of the individuality of Zarathustra; he is the individuality who has gathered up the greatest earthly experience through repeated lives on earth. And on the other side is the Buddha stream, which continuously remained connected, even in the last recapitulation in the sixth century before Christ, with the sphere of Paradise, with the godlike forces in human nature.

Zarathustra, Hermes and Moses

The founder of the primeval Persian religion—Zarathustra himself—is essentially the bearer and shaper of the entire earthly stream right up to the Christ event. If we follow Rudolf Steiner's description of Zarathustra's development as far as the Christ event, we discover that the one who gives the impulse for the Egyptian culture—Hermes Trismegistos, Hermes the three times Greatest—receives his astral body from Zarathustra.

The Hebrew religion arises through the fact that Zarathustra transfers his etheric body to Moses. Experiences in the domain of time are embedded into the etheric body, and thus it is that Moses is able to disclose the mysteries of evolution in time—especially in the book of Genesis. The astral body is the focal point of the forces spread out simultaneously in space. This is how Hermes is able to dedicate himself in the Egyptian religion more to the astrological mysteries of space. 'Astral body' of course means 'star body'.

Thus we see that Zarathustra was essentially involved in the origin of the religion of the Egyptian era through *Hermes* and the religion of Judaism through *Moses*.

At about the same time as the Buddha was incarnated in India, that is, in the sixth century before Christ, Zarathustra was incarnated anew in Chaldea, where again an encounter with Jewish culture took place through the captivity of the Jews in Babylon. In this incarnation Zarathustra was called *Zaratas* or *Nazaratos*. Zarathustra's following incarnation was then in Jesus of Nazareth of the St Matthew Gospel who, in his thirtieth year, became the Christ bearer.

There is an important statement in the Gospel which, in its archetypal imagery, can best be referred to Zarathustra's post-Atlantean development. What we have seen is that Zarathustra is the one who forms humanity's religions one after another, so that they all take their part in enabling the *incarnation of the Sun Being* to come about as a synthesis of all the forces of *love* for the earth and of the task of making the transformation of the earth the true religion of humankind.

It says in the Gospel: 'Thou shalt love the Lord thy God with all thy *strength*, with all thy *mind*, with all thy *soul* and with all thy heart or *spirit*' (see Mark 12:30).

The translations vary. Four things are being spoken about here. But first of all it says, 'You shall love the Lord *thy* God—that is, the God of the ego. Otherwise why does it say 'thy' God and not 'our' God? It is not speaking of 'our' God but of 'thy' God, the God of the individual ego. It is saying, 'You shall devote all your strength to the unfolding of the ego,' knowing that the overall plan the Godhead has envisaged for human beings is that each human being shall become more and more an ego.

This process of becoming truly human comes to expression in a fourfold way: 'You shall devote all the forces of the *physical body* to becoming truly human' ('with all thy *strength*'). 'You shall devote all the forces of your *etheric body* to this humanizing process.' The etheric body is the body of formative and thought forces ('with all thy mind'). 'You shall devote all the forces of your soul, all the forces of your *astral body* to the God of the ego. You shall devote all your soul forces to becoming more and more of an ego being in the course of time' ('with all thy soul').

The fourth is the *ego* itself, where the unifying ruler of your soul forces becomes more and more of a real experience ('with all your heart'; the ego, the spirit comes to expression in the blood). The religious development of the ego consists in this: what is, to begin with, the 'lower' ego (the soul in the actual sense) unites in a more and more real way with the 'higher' ego, so that the forces of egoism of the lower ego become transformed to a greater and greater extent into the forces of love of the higher ego.

Love thy God with Strength, Mind, Soul and Spirit

This important statement in the Gospels epitomizes the actual development of the individuality of Zarathustra as the founder of those pre-Christian religions which ascribed value to the earth. It completely sums up the evolution of the religions of humanity. Zarathustra is *the* individuality who, in the post-Atlantean era, achieves in an exemplary way what is contained in this Gospel statement.

Jesus of Nazareth, who utters this statement, is the reincarnated Zarathustra himself who, in his thirtieth year, withdrew his ego in order to make available to the Christ his threefold sheath—the physical, etheric and astral body. From out of this threefold sheath of Zarathustra, now indwelt by the Christ Being himself, there sounds forth to the whole of humankind the word of *fourfold love* for the forces of the ego to be acquired on the earth, for the experience of the godlike nature of the human ego: 'Love *thy* God (the God of the ego) with all thy strength (physical body); with all thy mind (etheric body); with thy whole soul (astral body); with thy whole heart (ego).' In this statement the Sun Being expresses the way in which the human being—every human being—can make possible the incarnation of the Logos: by imitating what Zarathustra's own development demonstrated with such archetypal imagery.

In very fact Zarathustra devoted his *ego-spirit* to the evolution of the ego-forces by being the first person in the ancient Persian culture to perceive and to venerate the Being of the Ego in the Sun. He became the first to understand humanity's evolution to be a challenge and a call to cultivate the power of the ego and, with the help of the earth's forces, make it more and more real.

Later on Zarathustra accomplishes the second part of this statement from the Gospels: Love the God of the ego with all thy *mind*. Zarathustra devoted all the forces of his etheric body, the forces of thought, to the cultivation of the ego forces in humankind in the sense that after his death he gave his etheric body, which had remained intact, to *Moses*. This was how the Hebraic culture, the Jewish religion, arose. And the third: Zarathustra devoted his *soul*, the entire forces of his astral body, in the most actual sense to the development of the human ego, in that he gave his astral body to *Hermes*, the founder of the Egyptian religion.

At the turning-point of time, when Zarathustra was born in Bethlehem, he was capable of devoting his physical body also, all his *strength*, to the evolution of the human ego.

Thus in an absolutely literal, spiritually real sense we have, in this Gospel statement, a synthesis on the one hand of the post-Atlantean evolution of the individuality of Zarathustra, and on the other hand of the religions of humankind in so far as they comprise the stream of ego development, the stream of devotion to the earth. 'Love thy God with all thy strength, with all thy mind, with thy whole soul, with thy whole spirit.' This fourfold statement does not mean more or less the same thing four times over. These sacred scriptures of humankind are extremely exact. They are written in the special terminology of esotericism, which one has to decipher in order to understand them at all. They presuppose a science of the supersensible.

Then the immediately following statement is: 'and love thy neighbour as thyself'. Loving the God of the ego is the same thing as loving the human being, for through developing the ego in a positive way human beings become more and more god-enfilled.

A Comparative Study of Religions and the 'True' Religion

We see, therefore, in what way the actual synthesis and harmony of all the religions in the history of humankind comes about—in fact in quite a different way than is often supposed today. In today's very widespread 'comparative study of religions' the usual aim is to compare the various religions from the point of view of their message, their theoretical content. People stress the particular truths common to all religions, by omitting the differences. They try to reconcile the religions by saying: Fundamentally all the religions in the world say the same thing.

Where Rudolf Steiner is concerned, his concept of the unity of all humanity's religions is quite different. From his standpoint the crux of the matter is to grasp the actual evolution of humankind and of each human being in the course of the millennia throughout their repeated earth lives. In this perspective the primary consideration is not theoretical 'truths' but *actual development*, i.e. what each human being *becomes* in the course of his incarnations. The unity, the wholeness of religions can only be the human being himself in the unity of his development seen as a whole.

Rudolf Steiner also has quite a different concept of 'true religion'. In the abstract and theoretically absolute sense there is no 'true religion'. What does exist is that at any given time and on every level of development human beings perform religious practices which are either *timely* or *untimely*. What is right for the time is the only religious practice that can possibly be good, and therefore 'true' and 'beautiful' in the sense that it is *beneficial to human beings*.

So we can say: at any given point of evolution religion can only be true and good if it promotes the next stage of development the times require. What is right for each time is constantly changing because human beings themselves are in a constant process of development.

Seen in this light human beings are called upon in the course of time—as we have already mentioned—to realize *in their own being* the actual synthesis of all religions. Initially this happens by way of a period of preparation in which they exercise the religious or the divine dimensions of their being *one after another*, so that their ego forces may be developed to the point where they become more and more capable of weaving all these aspects of human nature, through their own individual initiative, into an *integrated* harmony and synthesis within their own being. Thus through their own achievement human beings bring it about that the times are fulfilled, because through them and in them all the separate stages unite and come alive in the present moment.

The divine guidance of humankind makes use of the help of the great initiates who can unite with it so as to shape the cultural and other conditions on the earth to enable the religious stage necessary for the time to come about.

In the period of preparation the gods and the initiates have to take the shaping of religion and of the religions into their own hands, because it is only with their help that individual human beings will become more and more mature and capable of realizing the fulfilment of the times, in that religion becomes less and less a following of outer instruction and more and more a taking up of responsibility, out of their own inner freedom, for their own future potential. This is the way being human will become humanity's religion of the future.

The Union of the Two Streams in Jesus of Nazareth

At the turning-point of time the Buddha and the Zarathustra streams became one in Jesus of Nazareth. All the forces which had been awakened in human beings through the various religions were united in bodily incarnation in a spiritually alive way in his person. This is indicated in the St Luke Gospel when his parents do not recognize their twelve-year-old son when they find him teaching the scribes in the temple. He had in fact become quite a different person.

In the Luke Jesus child all the forces of humanity's heavenly innocence were embodied. The other spiritual stream, which had initially to develop separately for twelve years, united then and became one with these forces of the Luke child. The new element which then came to light, and

which could only fill his parents with the greatest aston-
ishment, was that this child now showed great intelligence
in the way in which he spoke to and answered the scribes.
This fact shows that the Zarathustra individuality, the ego
of Zarathustra, had now united with the Luke boy. In Jesus
of Nazareth the two great religious streams of the post-
Atlantean era were actually united, the Buddha stream and
the Zarathustra stream.

This human being—Jesus of Nazareth—can in the most
actual sense be regarded as the embodied synthesis of all
the religions of humankind. In him all the longing of
humankind to reconnect with the spiritual realm—to find
salvation—will be lived through again in all its denominational practices.

I asked the question previously: what further development is Buddha passing through since he entered the
spiritual world at his death six centuries before Christ? We
can now follow the Buddha stream further by looking at the
Buddha's development in Christian times. At the time he
became Buddha his whole life and teaching could be
summed up in the four great truths he expounded after his
enlightenment. They are the four well-known truths of
Buddhism.

The *first* truth says that life is suffering, all life is suffering:
birth is suffering, illness is suffering, growing old is
suffering, death is suffering. The *second* great truth says that
the origin and cause of suffering is the thirst for existence,
the desire for earthly embodiment, which brings the human
being to unite with matter over and over again. The *third*
great truth refers to the necessary release from suffering,
which human beings will attain by extinguishing the thirst
for existence and therefore no longer having to incarnate.
The *fourth* great truth is the path along which the human
being arrives at purifying himself, ridding himself of every
desire for the flesh, overcoming all suffering and no longer
needing to incarnate.

This path, the path of abolishing the thirst for existence, is the *eightfold* path already mentioned. It consists of eight basic exercises which the human being has constantly to perform to overcome the thirst for existence. Buddha passes through death with this basic attitude and consciousness, for this teaching was the content of the enlightenment he attained before his death in his twenty-ninth year. Our question now is: what further development does the Buddha pass through?

The Buddha at the Turning-point of Time

We can follow his further development only with spiritual, supersensible perception. Rudolf Steiner claims that it is possible to meet the Buddha about five centuries later at the turning-point of time, when he unites with the Christ bearer, Jesus of Nazareth.

In the St Luke Gospel we are told that a host of angels appears to the shepherds in the field, proclaiming that the Saviour has been born. This host of angels is a real visual imagination of the nirmanakaya of the Buddha, the Buddha's 'body of transfiguration'. There appears to the shepherds in the field, in a supersensible, spiritually real form, the Buddha himself, who has evolved further and is now about to unite all his forces with those of the Christ event.

Then we are told about the elderly Simeon who takes the small child into his arms and is thankful that the salvation of the world is at hand. Simeon is portrayed by Rudolf Steiner as the reincarnation of Asita, who was also an elderly person during the Buddha's lifetime in the sixth century before Christ, and who expressed his sadness at that time because he was not yet able to see the salvation of the world. The same individuality can now die and pass into the spiritual world comforted, because his eyes have beheld the salvation of humankind. John the Baptist's sermon in the St Luke's Gospel also bears an out-and-out Buddhist character.

Spiritual guidance of humanity brings about the unifying of religion in this spiritually real way. The Buddha unites his actual forces with the being of Jesus of Nazareth.

The Buddha and the Essenes: the Illusion of Separateness

Later on, over the course of six years, from his twenty-fourth until his thirtieth year, Jesus of Nazareth had frequent and intensive contact with the Essenes of those times, and was confronted with what still existed in humanity of the Buddhistic outlook.

In those days the Essenes, as also the Therapeuts in Egypt, lived in Palestine like Buddhist monks in the sense that they put into practice in the highest degree, through an ascetic lifestyle and the strict rules of their order, what the Buddha had preached six centuries before.

During these years, in which Jesus of Nazareth also had to experience Buddhism in the form in which it existed at that time among the ascetic Essenes, he once had a supersensible vision in which the Buddha himself appeared to him and told him that he himself had now become capable of seeing the error inherent in his former teaching.

The Buddha tells Jesus of Nazareth that the error in his teaching was to demand of human beings that they should all become Buddhist monks. If that were to happen, however, if for example sexual abstinence were practiced by everybody, the human race would soon die out. This means that his religion and teaching cannot be realized in practice.

Through this conversation with the spiritual being of Buddha Jesus of Nazareth learns something very important which is of paramount significance for the evolution of religion and for humanity's religious outlook. He learns that even though these Essenes may have had very good personal intentions by aspiring to a real connection with the spiritual world through distancing themselves from the rest of humankind by means of their asceticism, something was nevertheless missing. What they lacked was an awareness of the fact that humankind is a unity and all human beings are part of one another, and that it is objectively impossible that one single human being be saved and redeemed without all human beings being redeemed. The Buddhist life view lacked an awareness — which was typical of the preparatory, pre-Christian character of this stream — of the fact that the whole of humankind is a single organism. Not one single member of humankind can be saved unless he or she is working towards redeeming *all* human beings.

Jesus of Nazareth made the disconcerting discovery that even the teaching of the Essenes contained a great amount of egoistic illusion. These people were endeavouring, in a personal and therefore egoistic way, to get to the spiritual world themselves without really caring about the salvation of others. This is due to the illusion of being separate from the rest of humankind, without recognizing that the whole significance of our further evolution consists in this separation, caused by the Fall, having to be undone through all human beings becoming one in a spiritually real way.

The Buddha confesses to Jesus of Nazareth that he had this illusion. And he tells him that he has developed further in the spiritual world after his death through the very fact of seeing through this grave illusion. For Jesus of Nazareth, who is the personified longing of *all* humanity for redemption, this conversation becomes a decisive turning-point. It happened actually shortly before the baptism in the Jordan.

For him the inner turning-point consists in his becoming conscious of the fundamental illusion of separateness and egoism through the very fact that he learns from the Buddha himself that an individual can only be truly human by having love for all people, and that nobody can be saved in a state of separation from the rest of humankind. This universal message, involving the welfare of the whole of humankind, of which Jesus of Nazareth now becomes fully conscious, and which was also due to the help of the Buddha, was the final preparation enabling Jesus of Nazareth to make himself a vessel for humankind to offer itself to the Christ. It is the human vessel of true compassion and true love, for which the Buddha had longed, and which now for the first time becomes an actual reality in Jesus because it embraces the *whole* of creation.

The arising of a *human being* who realized in himself the religions of all peoples, through universal love, was the completion of all the religious preparation for the entry of the *godlike* Being of Love into humankind. Through the forces arising out of sharing through *compassion* the suffering caused by the Fall and separation, Jesus offered, out of his longing for redemption, the whole of humankind to the Christ. Christ offered to humankind all the forces of *love* which annul all separation by the bringing together again of all people.

The Buddha After the Coming of the Christ: Barlaam and Josaphat

We can follow in broad sweeps the further development of the Buddha after the coming of the Christ. There is a medieval Christian legend, the legend of Barlaam and Josaphat, which tells of how Barlaam, who is a Christian, converts Josaphat, an Indian prince, to Christianity. (The name Josaphat is a modification of *bodasat, bodhisattva*.) This legend can be traced back to a John of Damascus, and is also cited in the 'Legenda Aurea'. Rudolf Steiner refers a number of times to this medieval legend to show that something absolutely real and true is being told here in the form of a story, namely, the important fact that in the spiritual world after his death the Buddha has linked up with the Christian stream.

In the Middle Ages there was, at least in some people, a consciousness of the manner in which the union of religions happened in actual reality — by way of the development of human beings and spiritual entities themselves. Buddhism is taken further by the living Buddha himself in such a way that it merges into Christianity in a spiritually real way. However, we must always distinguish between Christianity as a spiritual, mystical fact and the outer form it assumes at any given period in human culture and in the religious practice of the time.

This wonderful legend is saying that from the spiritual world the living Buddha is participating in the activities of the Christ impulse after the Christian era has begun. The Buddha has been 'converted' to Christianity; he has become convinced that the incarnation of the Sun Being has not established one more religion among others but that it represents the coming together of all religions.

The different religions of humankind are united in the course of time by the founders of the religions themselves. What they called into being in their time, among their own people, they bring into unity through their own further evolution.

The Buddha 'on Mars' and Francis of Assisi

Rudolf Steiner speaks of the fact that Christian Rosenkreutz, who plays a decisive part in the evolution of esoteric Christianity, gave to the Buddha at the beginning of the seventeenth century the task of working supersensibly in the Mars sphere. That was the beginning of the period when a spirit of combat, of aggressiveness, was constantly on the increase among humankind, because they were becoming more and more materialistic, were sinking further and further into the realm where the ruling law was that of being in competition one with another. In the materialistic realm human beings are descending ever more deeply into the experience of egoism, competition and opposition.

To remedy this the great teacher of love and compassion, the supersensible being of Buddha, was asked by Christian Rosenkreutz to unite with the Mars sphere so that human beings, on returning to a new incarnation, would have their aggressiveness tempered and softened in the Mars sphere. Thus according to Rudolf Steiner the Buddha has been carrying out a cosmic sacrifice in the Mars sphere since the seventeenth century to tame the warring spirit of egoism, in imitation of the Christ Being's loving sacrifice.

Each human being, as he passes through the Mars sphere on the way to a new incarnation, receives from the Buddha forces of compassion and love to overcome belligerence through love and gentleness. The Buddha helps each one of us to transform aggression into kindness and good will.

The example of the development of Francis of Assisi is closely connected with the Buddha stream. Rudolf Steiner describes how, before his incarnation as Francis of Assisi, he had experienced a Buddhist incarnation in a Mystery School at the Sea of Colchis. The Mysteries of Colchis were inspired by the spirit of Buddhism. A twofold initiation took place there. The first stage was more Buddhistic, and this was open to all the pupils. At this stage the central focus was on the teaching of compassion and love. The higher stage consisted of an actual encounter with the Sun Being in the spiritual world.

Francis of Assisi, who had undergone both stages, bore within himself the actual union of Buddhism and Christianity. Francis of Assisi's universal love can be regarded as Buddhistic yet at the same time deeply Christian. The phenomenon of Francis of Assisi can only really be understood if we take the actual evolution he passed through in his previous incarnation into account, and we know in what way the Buddha himself participated in this evolution.

With the aid of this example we see that we cannot say one particular religion is true and another false, but that the essential thing is always to recognize the positive, spiritually real contribution of every single religion to human evolution.

The Pre-Christian Experience of the Ego: Buddhism, Hellenism and Hebraism

An important matter we ought to look at before we come to speak about the religion of Judaism is that of the *ego* and ego consciousness before Christ. It is bound up with another matter, namely, in what way the Christ Being brings about the culmination and the conclusive validity of the ego forces in humankind.

The best transition we can have to the subject of Judaism is to look at the evolution of ego consciousness in pre-Christian humankind, because the evolution of the ego is a very special factor of Judaism.

In the fifth lecture of the cycle *From Jesus to Christ* Rudolf Steiner summarizes, from the point of view of the forces of the ego, the kind of consciousness existing in humankind a few centuries before the coming of the Christ. He points to three basic streams representative at that time of the whole of humankind.

The first stream is *paganism*, which is represented by Hellenism; the second is *Judaism*, ancient Hebraism, and the third is *Buddhism*. Rudolf Steiner describes with reference to these three basic streams the situation regarding ego consciousness in humankind shortly before the coming of the Christ. This survey also enables us to understand humanity's religious situation at the time. The way people related to the ego shows us in the clearest possible way how necessary it was for redemption to be offered to humankind as the answer of divine beings to the religious longing of human beings.

Nagasena to Milinda: The Ego is an Illusion

When we look at the original teaching of the Buddha we find that the fundamental message of Buddhism is that the ego is a great illusion. If we are focusing on pre-Christian Buddhism we do not include all that has been added to it later. Many people know Buddhism today only in the form it has acquired in the course of the past two thousand years.

This explains why many people would object today to hearing it said that Buddhism regards the ego as the greatest illusion. What is meant here is what the Buddha taught in his lifetime in the sixth century before Christ, and not what has entered Buddhism in later times through the fact that even in the Buddhist culture people have had a clearer and clearer experience of the reality of the ego through their very participation in the general evolution of humankind.

In the sixth century before Christ the Buddha himself describes the ego as an illusion. In the famous conversation between King Milinda and the wise Nagasena the latter endeavours to prove to the king in what sense the ego is an illusion and not a reality. He uses the example of a carriage. He asks the king how he came there. The king says he came by carriage. Nagasena asks him to tell him what is actually real about the carriage. The wheels are real, and so are the shaft and the body – in fact all the parts you can enumerate are real.

It is certainly not true, he argues, that in addition to the parts there is a further reality in that all these parts can be summarized by the word 'carriage'. This does not add a new reality. If you have all the parts then you have the whole carriage, all of it. And when you say the word 'carriage' you do not mean a new reality, for it does not signify a new reality at all—for only the various parts are real. For the sake of convenience you do not want to count them all up every time, so you have invented a collective noun, the word 'carriage'. However, this word does not correspond to reality, because only the parts are real.

Other examples are also used to prove that no reality appertains to the so-called 'ego', a collective noun. We could also ask whether it would be at all possible to 'prove' the opposite, i.e. to prove that the ego is a reality, that it is something real.

We mentioned earlier on that the only thing that can be proved to be real is something that is actually experienced. The proof that trees exist makes sense only after you have experienced the reality of trees. So what is the Buddha trying to say with his 'proof' that the ego is an illusion? What is actually being proved is the fact that in the case of the Buddha himself—as with any average person of that time in the East—a real experience of the ego did not as yet exist. In this sense we can say that the proof the wise Nagasena gave King Milinda was 'correct'.

If we are dealing with people who are hardly capable of experiencing ego-nature as something spiritually real the proof will point solely to the fact that the person in question does not yet experience himself as an ego. In this sense the original teaching of the Buddha in the sixth century before Christ is 'true', because it is the real proof of the fact that the very thing that the whole of evolution is geared to bring about in slow stages—a real experience of the ego—was still lacking in the orientals of those times.

When the ego is included in conscious human experience as a real spiritual entity and not as a theoretical abstraction, then the word 'I' —we can think of the philosopher Fichte— means a reality with the greatest possible content and potentiality. In short, we can say that in the Buddha's pre-

Christian activity and teaching an experience of the reality of the human ego was still lacking. Nor was it the task of pre-Christian religions to introduce into humankind a conclusive experience of the ego, but rather to prepare for its coming.

Achilles to Odysseus: Better a Beggar on Earth . . .

Let us pass on to *Hellenism*. We need only think of personalities such as Pericles, Phidias, Socrates, Plato or Aristotle: human beings are definitely now beginning to experience themselves as personalities enclosed in themselves. The human being now sees himself not only as a vehicle for the activity of gods but as an independent fountainhead of forces. There is no doubt about it that the concept of the ego begins to signify an actual experience. The human being is clearly beginning to experience himself as a separate and integrated ego. In the age of Greece there was the other factor, namely, that a Greek owed his ego experience — the fact of his feeling himself to be a personality enclosed in himself — to his *physical* body. What Achilles says to Odysseus in the eleventh canto of the *Odyssey* tells us something profound about Greek civilization. Odysseus has descended into the underworld and attempts to comfort the dead Achilles by telling him that his fame will live forever in human memory. Achilles, however, does not find this of any help, and answers with the statement Rudolf Steiner often quoted: 'Better a beggar on earth [where one is in possession of a physical body], than a king in the land of shades.'

It was a tragic fact to a Greek that on laying aside his body his ego-nature — the experience of himself as a personality enclosed in itself — was imperilled to such an extent that he could no longer experience himself as a whole person but only as a shadow of a human being. This really was so. It was not something a Greek just imagined but a reality. The dead lived in a state of dimmed consciousness.

This shadowlike quality of consciousness which a human being of those days experienced after death is a dimension of 'hell', of the darkness into which the Christ descended in his 'descent into hell' to bring light there and to enable human beings to have a clear ego consciousness even without their body.

It remains a fact that in the last centuries before Christ a Greek's self-awareness was so dependent on his body that his ego consciousness was seriously jeopardized by the circumstance that everyone is destined to lay his body aside.

This is the only way we can understand how tremendously tragic the experience was which a Greek went through as he wrestled in his consciousness with the mystery of death. Nothing ranked as more precious to a Greek than his physical body. He glorified in the form of his body to such an extent in his artistic creations that he gave all the gods a human form. At the same time he realized that it was just this body — which was of the greatest value, because a human being owed to it the greatest thing, namely, the experience of his ego as the crown of his humanity — this body, of all things, that had to be laid aside at death.

Thus we see in the awakening feeling for the ego in Greek civilization the arising in human consciousness of the great *problem of death* in preparation for the mystery of the death and the resurrection of the Christ. The Greeks knew about death, but the forces were not yet there to enable them to go through it as victors and to experience a full resurrection of their total ego-nature in a purely spiritual condition. To start with it remained such that the human being had to go through a considerable darkening of his consciousness when he laid aside his body.

Where the aspect of Greek religion regarding the

experiencing and the reality of the ego was concerned, we can say: in human beings there was an actual experience of the ego, even though it was only a rudimentary one. This was a considerable step forward compared to Buddhism. A Greek could not possibly have said that the ego was the greatest illusion. He would even have said that the experience of self as a self-contained personality was a human being's greatest asset. But the tremendous tragedy was that this was due to the physical body and that death put the whole matter in doubt.

Job's Wife to Job: Renounce Jehovah and Die

Let us pass on to Judaism. This is entirely different again. Here, too, there arises an actual awareness and conscious-ness of the ego. The God of the Jewish people even bears the name of the ego. Yahveh means 'I am'. I am he who was, who is and who is to come. This means: I am the oneness in the succession of time, I am the identity of the ego which remains unchanging in the metamorphosis manifesting in the course of time: 'Ehjeh, asher, ehjeh'.

In the realm of the soul there is nothing which remains unchanging. Every condition is constantly passing through change. But thanks to the Jehovah forces a Hebrew acquired the capacity to experience his own permanent identity, to experience himself as a being who maintained his identity. In the infinite variability of the soul there was the experi-ence of something which remained the same, and that was the ego. I am the same person I was yesterday, I am the same person I am today, and I am the same person I shall be tomorrow.

This fact of remaining identical to oneself in the changes coming about in the course of time is the essence of the experience of the ego which was ushered in by the Semitic people but appeared in a quite unique form in Judaism. The

experience of the ego in humankind is the origin of monotheism. For monotheism arises when human beings begin
to feel themselves as a unity within a multiplicity.

Whilst there is still no experience of the ego, human
beings feel themselves solely as a multiplicity, a multiplicity
of forces which, perhaps outside themselves, are brought
together into a unity, possibly in the consciousness of a
divine Being, without human beings being consciously
aware of it.

When the Godhead is understood to be monotheistic,
then a monotheistic experience arises in human beings. But
one can also say, the other way round: where a monotheistic
experience of the self arises in a person's ego-nature the
Godhead will also be understood to be monotheistic. They
belong together. The human being is now beginning to
experience himself as a unity, as an absolute authority who,
attributing to himself the multiplicity of his inner impulses,
refers them to himself and takes responsibility for them.

Although, due to Jehovah's influence, the experience of
the ego arises more clearly among the Jews than among the
Greeks, even in this case the ego experience is not yet a
purely spiritual one in the sense that it owes its origin to two
factors, one, the body, and the other, the soul.

It comes from the body in that Jehovah, as the God of the
ego, is present and active in the blood flowing through the
generations. It is solely due to the fact that a Jew is
embedded with his bodily nature in Jehovah's bloodstream,
shares through his bodily nature in the forces of Jehovah
pulsating through the blood, that he could be educated at
all in the mysteries of the ego. That is the bodily aspect.

The soul factor is that this ego-nature is initially being
given to a Jewish person in the form of the law of Moses. It
has not yet become an individual matter. The ego forces
come about to begin with by means of the Ten Commandments, through the fulfilment of the law of all the people, at
a time when human beings still had a group-soul nature.

Each member of the Jewish people is embedded in the forces of the physical blood and in the soul experience of the law which is the law governing the process of becoming an ego. They owed their ego experience entirely to Jehovah and hardly as yet to themselves. Therefore Job's wife says to her husband (and we shall come back to this again), 'Renounce Jehovah and die ... If you cut yourself off from all that Jehovah causes to happen in you, there will be nothing left and you will cease suffering.'

The evolution of ego consciousness in humankind in these three cultural and religious streams is representative of the whole of humankind. In Buddhism there was as yet no ego awareness. In the Far East, in the eastern religion, ego awareness was not yet possible. Among both the Greek people and the Jews there was the first beginnings of an ego awareness in preparation for the turning of the times. But this ego awareness was only a rudimentary one in the sense that it was not yet purely spiritual and individual. To become a reality, to continue even after death, it had to become entirely independent of the body.

This rudimentary ego awareness owed its existence to the forces of the body and the soul in which the Godhead, not the human being, was at work. It was a God-given, instinctive ego awareness. It was still dependent on the body and on the group soul.

This condition of human consciousness shows us more than anything else that the mystery of the ego represented the focal point of the religious evolution of humankind. The religion of all of humanity was a movement towards achieving the full validity of ego awareness, the spiritual awareness of human individuality.

4

THE MISSION OF JUDAISM

In the evolution of humankind before the turning-point of time there was a particular people with a particular mission: the Jewish, the ancient Hebrew people. The mission of this people is documented in the Old Testament, in a text that has played a decisive role in the history of humankind, and also in the history of Christianity up till now, because the Christian Bible contains not only the New Testament but also the Old Testament.

Judaism deserves a special place in the series of pre-Christian religions. The first thing we can say about the special mission of Judaism is the fact that among this people, the Jewish people, there arose for the very first time in humankind on the one hand a *moral* consciousness and on the other a consciousness of *historical* development.

Through this appearance of a consciousness of a moral element and of a historical element Judaism can be regarded as a polarity compared to everything else which existed among humankind in those days, especially in the last centuries before the coming of the Christ.

With regard to all the religions outside Judaism—in paganism and in all eastern religions—there was as yet no moral or historical consciousness; the course of events was regarded more as cyclic, more as though the Godhead and nature were constantly bringing about an eternal repetition of the same. The life of a plant was for them the archetypal phenomenon of the course of events—the old plant containing the seed for the new plant which then repeats, according to the same laws, what took place in the previous one.

Repetition of the Same and Progressive Evolution

The course of events in both nature and in human beings was regarded everywhere else except in Judaism as cyclic. It was assumed that all phenomena — even on the human level — presented an eternal repetition of the same, leaving no room for 'progress' of any kind, for new impulses or for 'creations out of nothingness' which presuppose freedom. Whenever a cycle came to an end it was repeated in the new cycle in exactly the same way. The whole thing simply began all over again without anything essentially new being added.

The evolution of the ancient Hebrew people was quite different. The God of the people, called Jehovah, brought it about that there arose for the first time a consciousness of history and an awareness of human moral development within the course of history. They recognized progressive stages in evolution. Human beings are called upon by the Godhead to take a more and more conscious and responsible part in the whole forward course of the earth and humankind.

They are called upon to understand more and more clearly the nature of the responsibility arising for them in the course of this entire evolution. This presupposes that human beings must gradually acquire the ability to become aware of the meaning and purpose of evolution altogether.

This will also make human beings accountable from a moral point of view. They will learn to bear responsibility for their destiny, which is to be consciously creative. A consciousness of humanity's moral freedom announces itself in the ancient Hebrew people through their declaration of moral accountability with regard to the law. There arises an awareness of sin and evil.

Right at the beginning of the Old Testament, in the first book of Moses, the Genesis, the creation is presented from the standpoint of evolution in time. We see immediately that we are dealing with historical evolution, with the story of *progressive development*. Evolutionary goals are set which will not tolerate any cyclic repetition of the same.

If Human Beings Become Active then God Can 'Rest'

From the start there has always been the awareness that the final and highest goal towards which everything is tending is man himself. Man was created on the sixth day as the culmination of the whole of creation. The fact that after creating the human being Jehovah rested on the seventh day is an indication that human beings are in a sense called upon to *continue* God's activity.

The Godhead may now 'withdraw' with regard to the things human beings themselves will 'take on' in the course of time. Where humanity is concerned the Godhead cannot continue to be the sole creator. Just as in the first days of creation it was a matter of being active entirely on his own, so, after humankind had been created on the sixth day, the opposite was the case, and the Godhead had to 'rest', on the seventh day, which is the meaning of the word 'Sabbath'.

Human beings are the final creation just because the Godhead can make way for them. They are created in the image of the Godhead, which means they themselves are capable of working creatively in a godlike way. In the course of time it is open to them to lay claim to a sphere of action and take over their own evolution in freedom and love.

The Jewish Kabbala, the ancient Hebrew Mystery teaching, speaks of 'sim-sum', of the 'fasting' of God. Jehovah 'fasts' on the seventh day. This exceedingly beautiful picture of the fasting of Jehovah points to the same mystery. Where humankind are concerned the Godhead wants to 'fast', knowing that he has to give way. He has to renounce his own 'almighty' activity to make way for humanity, so that humankind can have their share of the responsibilty of the creativeness in the whole of evolution.

This moral consciousness developing on the basis of history, this consciousness of the evolutionary process, is in total contrast to the consciousness of going round and round in the same cycle for ever, as exists in the East and also in the Greek religion. If, for instance, we look at the *Iliad* and the *Odyssey* of Homer we see that human beings do not as yet have a moral awareness in the actual sense. Even the gods are described similarly to other natural happenings. Even Zeus acts in a way we might consider morally dubious.

But Homer did not have this moral view of things, either. In his view the gods were just as they happened to be, no less so than anything else in the world. The thought categories of the moral qualities of Good and Evil, which arise for the first time in Jewish-Christian consciousness, existed as yet nowhere else. For a moral awareness of Good and Evil presupposes the exercise of human freedom, even if this is still at a rudimentary stage.

Abraham's Unique Bodily Structure

Let us see in what way and by means of which evolutionary stages this historic moral consciousness came about.

The call to Abraham, and his mission, was the first great step. He plays an important role in the transition from oriental cyclic consciousness to the Hebrew historic/moral consciousness. What was so special and totally new about him was that he was the first human being whose physical *brain* received, through Jehovah's influence, a certain particular structure.

The beginning of Jehovah's activity among the Hebrew people was this moment when Abraham became the first human being to have a differently constructed brain from any of his predecessors. Initially it concerned the quality of the bodily structure as the basis for all that would follow later among the Hebrew people in the realm of soul and also of spirit. In the case of Abraham a physical body was for the first time so transformed that right into the finest fibres the physical brain was differently shaped from other people's. Abraham was the first person to possess the kind of brain that enabled him, even if only in a very rudimentary way, to experience what was clearly deductive, discursive thinking.

Traditional sources tell us of this in various ways: for example, that Abraham was the founder of arithmetic. This points to the fact that before the time of Abraham people could not even count because counting presupposes pacing things out, one after another, in discursive thinking. This capacity can arise only at the expense of being able to experience everything all at once in one comprehensive glance. Now, for the first time, separate elements are experienced in succession, and these have to be added together. This adding up is the beginning of discursive, logical thinking.

The word *manas* is in Sanskrit the archetypal word for the ability to think, Latin *mens*, and in English the word for man. In ancient Hebrew *manah* means 'counting'. Here we have the fact of this manas force becoming in Abraham the ability to count arithmetically. Jehovah establishes the mission he wants to accomplish through Abraham and his people by way of the fact of creating the bodily conditions necessary for this mission.

The next thing was to make Abraham himself aware of what his mission was. He had to realize that he was capable of doing what Jehovah expected of him, and what other people around him could not do. This is shown in the fact that he really is no longer at home in his old environment, and has to leave his homeland of Ur, in Chaldea. The Chaldean culture, which was the prevailing one up till Abraham's time, had now become out of date.

Because something absolutely new is coming about in Abraham that does not fit into the old ways, he has to leave his homeland and take his way to the west, as far as Canaan. We can see how the path of destiny of the ancient Hebrew people alternates between Chaldea and Egypt. Later on there is the sojourn in Egypt which Moses brought to an end.

Judaism can be seen as a transition from the third post-Atlantean cultural period—the cultural period of the Egyptians and the Chaldeans—to the fourth, the Graeco-Roman period, and when, at the turning-point of time, the Christ event occurs. The impulse of Judaism is the transition from the culture of the Egyptians and Chaldeans to this fourth, central cultural period.

This fact of having to withdraw, of having to be segregated, which started with Abraham, is a consistent part of the history of Judaism. The progenitor of the nation is taken out of Chaldea. Later on the whole people are taken out of Egypt, and later on still out of the Babylonian captivity. All these events took place to usher in what was new, the coming of the 'Messiah'.

Moses and the Ten Commandments – Attributes of Ego Development

The next decisive step in the development of Judaism is achieved through Moses. The Jehovah God is the God of the ego: 'I am he who was, who is and who is to come.' He works towards a clearer and clearer awakening of the ego consciousness in human beings. Just as Abraham was led out of Chaldea, Moses was led out of Egypt. Just as in Abraham the first ego-orientated *body* arose, in Moses there arose the *soul* of the ego: the law.

The Moses stage in the evolution of the Jewish people has

to do with the element of soul. Now it is no longer a matter of forming a special bodily structure but a special soul configuration which can take up the evolution in the direction of the ego forces, the Jehovah forces.

The impulse at the Abraham stage was the sacred command to keep the line of bodily descent pure, because Jehovah was a God who worked in the blood, in the generations. He is the God of Abraham, Isaac and Jacob. When we come to Moses we have to do with the mysteries of the soul, with everything the human being has to experience in his thinking, feeling and will as a partner of the Godhead. It is now a matter of the human being really understanding the law of Moses and respecting it. He can hold faith with Jehovah only by observing the law and implementing it. Just as the first foundation of Judaism is represented in the blood of the body, Moses now makes the Torah, the law, the soul foundation for the way the human being experienced himself inwardly.

The important question arises at this point: what is the nature of the Ten Commandments of Moses as a summing up of the law? What do the Ten Commandments signify?

In my opinion what Rudolf Steiner has said about the nature of the Ten Commandments belongs among the most beautiful treasures of his spiritual science. His fundamental statement is that the Ten Commandments are in reality ten attributes for the ego development of a human being. They represent the ten basic rules for experiencing the nature of the ego in a more and more real way, and for acquiring to a greater and greater extent the inner capacity to become aware of the responsibility belonging to human beings for their own evolution and that of the earth.

Rudolf Steiner translates the first commandment (Exodus 20:2-6) as follows: 'I am the eternal, divine being whom you experience in yourself. I led you out of the land of Egypt, where you could not experience me in you. Henceforth you shall not put other gods above me. You shall not recognize as higher gods those who present to you an image of anything that appears above in the heavens, or that works out of the earth, or between heaven and earth. You shall not worship anything that is below the divine in yourself. For I am the eternal in you that works into your body and thus affects the coming generations. I am of divine nature working forth. If you do not recognize me as your God I shall pass away as your ego in your children, grandchildren and great-grandchildren, and their bodies will become waste. If you recognize me in you I shall live on as you unto the thousandth generation, and the bodies of your people shall prosper.'*

We can see from this rendering of the original text that the commandments of Jehovah's law work in the direction of awakening and fostering a human being's ego experience. Only by becoming more and more ego conscious, by experiencing him or herself as an independent and separate individuality will a human being become responsible in a moral sense.

Moses receives on Mount Sinai—initially as a divine revelation from outside—the tenfold law of ego development which can only attain its significance when it becomes alive in a person's inner being. For the ego is entirely inward—and this is why a Hebrew was not to make a graven image of Jehovah. Any kind of image would be an externalization, a contradiction of the purely inner soul experience of the ego. Greek art, by contrast, was, from beginning to end, an externalized portrayal. In the art of the Greeks, images are made of *all* the gods. This is why the Old Testament is riddled with opposition to paganism.

The transitional character of the mission of Moses also stems from the nature of the Ten Commandments as the manifestation of the laws of ego development. What Moses had received as divine revelation has to be taken into the

---

*See the lecture by Rudolf Steiner of 16 November 1908 in *The Ten Commandments and The Sermon on the Mount*, Anthroposophic Press, New York 1978.

inner being of every Jew until it becomes their own inner conviction. At that point Moses' role as intermediary becomes superfluous. We can understand therefore why Moses may not enter the Promised Land — the land where the ego works directly and independently.

Monotheism as Evidence of Human Self-awareness

The Jehovah revelation on Mount Sinai established at one and the same time a *monotheistic* consciousness in human-kind. As we have already mentioned, two things belong irrevocably together: the inner self-awareness of being a single, integrated ego and the conception of the Godhead as ego-endowed in the highest and most creative sense. As soon as the human being begins even in a rudimentary way to experience himself as a *single, integrated ego*, he cannot do otherwise than also recognize that the greatest and most essential quality of the Godhead is his oneness. In a sense Ludwig Feuerbach is right when he says that the human being can attribute to the Godhead only those qualities which he experiences as belonging in some way to himself, and that anything of which he has no experience does not exist for him. The Greek Protagoras had more or less also said this.

Why were the Greeks polytheists? This was because, in contrast to the Hebrews, they experienced in themselves the infinite *manifoldness of the soul* and hardly as yet the ego force which could integrate and master this manifoldness. Here again we see the essential difference between soul and spirit. *Soul* is infinite multiplicity and changeableness, a surging sea of drives, desires and passions. Nothing in the soul is lasting, everything is transient; nothing is objective and communicable, everything is subjective and experienced only personally. On the other hand *spirit* is unity and durability. Through the spirit of the ego multiplicity is mastered, because the ego is 'master'—Greek *Kupios*—of the soul forces.

The Greek gods are actual supersensible beings who rule the soul impulses in the human being and in the cosmos. For the ego people, the Jehovah people, it was therefore a question of life and death not to fall back into the superstitions of the polytheism of the heathens. Greek polytheism was a perpetual existential threat to the people of monotheism. If a human being stops experiencing himself as an integrated ego there is no question any more of any freedom or morality.

Through Jehovah's divine guidance a Jew was to have an ever more actual experience of himself as a responsible and kingly exemplification of the impulse that enabled him to bring into a unified whole the infinite multiplicity of his soul forces—his thoughts, his feelings and his aims. He was to experience himself as an ego: as an integrated force from which all his soul impulses originated.

The budding human ability to be aware of himself as an integrated divine creative being is based on the stream of monotheism.

Thou shalt make no image of thy God—of *thy* God, please note. This phrase 'of *thy* God' ought to be translated as 'of the God of the ego', for what does 'of thy God' mean? Wherever we have 'thy God' or 'my God, my God...' in the Old Testament we should always translate it with 'God of the ego'. Otherwise—if the importance of the people is that they are at the same time Jews—we would not be able to understand why it does not always say 'our God'.

The Law from Without and the Law from Within

The mission of Moses is of a transitional character because it lies in the nature of the law of ego development that in the course of evolution it has to cease to be a law applied from outside. The meaning of the law of Moses is fulfilled in the very abolishing of the law. Obedience to the law of the ego must bring human beings to the point of no longer needing a law governing from outside. The law revealed from outside must be transformed into a law of the inner being, of the *ego*. It needs to cease to be guidance from outside and change into guidance from within. The Torah needs to be transformed into the human being's most individual, innermost and *free will*. In the sphere of a human being's freedom every law as such is cancelled out, in fact raised to a higher level and fulfilled.

Arising from what has been said we can trace the progress of the Hebrew people according to the trinity of body, soul and spirit. In his book *Theosophy* and also in other places Rudolf Steiner emphasizes the importance of approach to this trinity, which supplies a thought structure for the understanding of all manner of phenomena including historical phenomena.

Jehovah is the *spirit* of the Jewish people, the spirit of the ego. In the impulse working in Abraham we see the arising of the essential first condition for the Jehovah impulse, a *body* capable of supporting an ego. Through Moses there arises the *soul* of the Jewish people; this is developed with the help of the law, and becomes more and more an inner force. In the course of this process the law increasingly loses the character of a group soul, of the soul of a people, and is increasingly individualized in the sense of the ego.

The incarnation of the I AM, of the total forces of the Logos in humankind and the earth, will represent the fulfilment of Jehovah's purpose. This gives to each human being the opportunity to make use of the aspects of the body and of the soul as a twofold condition to realize more and more in himself, in a totally individual way, both as an experience and as an activity, the essence of the 'I AM', which is the esoteric name for the Christ Being, the Sun Being, in the Gospel of St John.

The transitional character of the mission of Moses is

evident from the fact that Moses is actually unable to enter the Promised Land, and has to stay behind. Moses does not enter the Promised Land! This fact confronts us in the Old Testament as a riddle. The laws of ego development were given to him in the first place from outside as divine revelation. It could not have been any different to begin with. This relation to the law, however, is only an initial one, a temporary one.

When we are dealing with the law of ego development, of the developing freedom and independence of human beings then, as we have already said, it is in the nature of this law itself that its inherent character of being given from outside has to be overcome. The human being has to make this law his own possession, making it the subject of his own thinking to such an extent that he becomes more and more convinced of it, that it becomes the law of his own thinking itself, so that Jehovah's intentions become what he himself intends and wills out of the innermost core of his own individual ego being.

Elias and the Riddle of Job

There is another central figure in the Old Testament who actually solves for us the riddle of why Moses cannot enter the Promised Land. This figure is Elias. Moses and Elias are the two great milestones in the evolution of the Hebrew people. They also, according to the Gospels, appear one on each side of the Sun Being in the Transfiguration on Mount Tabor.

If we want to come closer to the mystery of Elias we must connect him with the riddle of the book of Job in the Old Testament. The book of Job has always been a crucial one not only in the history of the Jewish people but also in the whole text of the Old Testament. There have always been attempts to remove this book from the Old Testament. Many people regarded it as not belonging there.

Job's momentous question is at the same time a matter of

conscience at the deepest level for every person adhering to
the Jewish religion up to the present day. For the book of Job
tells us of a man who is devoted through and through to the
law of Moses, who is totally dedicated to the Torah.
Although Job is so faithful to Jehovah, everything goes
wrong for him. One misfortune occurs after another, so that
finally all his neighbours and especially his wife endeavour
to persuade him to doubt the honesty, even the existence of
Jehovah. We can see his wife as the expression of Job's own
soul. It is Job himself as a person of *soul*, who is still at the
Moses stage of the law, and he has not yet realized its
transitional character. The voice of his own Moses soul tells
him: If you reject your God you will die.

This expresses the deep conviction of every 'righteous',
law-abiding Jew, that he can experience his own existence
only by being embedded in the folk impulse of Jehovah. He
cannot experience himself as yet as an independent, individual ego being. He exists solely by virtue of Jehovah's
activity among his people. He experiences himself not as a
separate ego but as a member of his people. If he rejects
Jehovah he will disappear into nothingness.

Clinging in this way to Jehovah in the course of observing
the law was bound to lead him to the great temptation of
regarding the Moses character of the Torah, its character of
revelation, as a final stage. The temptation to remain at the
transitional stage, as though it were the final one, is
expressed in the fact that his dedication to the law and to
Jehovah become more and more externalized in the course
of time.

Let me quote a few sentences from Rudolf Steiner's
lecture of 14 December 1911 on the mission of the Prophet
Elias (from the cycle *Menschengeschichte im Lichte der Geis-
tesforschung**; this series of lectures is a wonderful survey of
fundamental impulses in the religions of humankind):

---

* Rudolf Steiner Verlag, Dornach 1983. Not translated into English.

The Jehovah religion, a revering of a supersensible God who can be characterized in no other way than by saying: He has no similarity with anything else except that invisible and supersensible element of which a human being becomes conscious when he observes his own ego. That supersensible element was there, yet it was understood in such a way that people endeavoured as it were to identify, by means of external phenomena of human life, in what way their Jehovah God was active. They had acquired a habit of saying: Jehovah works in such a way that he rewards people and shows that he is kindly disposed when outer nature flourishes in great abundance and life is easy. However, they were also in the habit of saying that their God Jehovah waxed wrath or was turning his back on human beings when such things as wars and famine occurred.

Trials as a Mark of God's Special Love

This is saying that the Jehovah impulse had become identified with external abundance and success, that is, no longer only with the constitution of their bodily nature or with soul experience associated with the law. It had even been externalized to a further degree. The Jehovah activity became identified with the outer occurrences in nature to the point where people said: If everything goes well around us, if everything of a material nature flourishes, that is a sign that Jehovah is well disposed towards us; if everything around us goes badly, and we have to suffer, that is a sign that Jehovah is turning his back on us.

We could of course say to this that the opposite also applies. The strength of the ego increases most of all when outer circumstances offer more resistence and hindrances. In difficult times one has to muster greater ego strength. On the other hand one tends to neglect the strength of the ego —

Jehovah! — when everything goes well around one, because one has less opportunity to awaken strong ego forces for meeting a situation if it is easy.

The mission of Elias is to be understood in this way. A deciding factor for his mission was the fact that Elias became active during a period of famine. The famine signified that it was a time when outer circumstances presented each individual ego among the Hebrew people with suffering and with trials no less than those of Job. With the entire nation plunged into this Job situation, Elias appeared bringing a solution opposite to the one brought by Job's wife. Elias is the new moral voice of Jehovah; this tells every Jew the opposite of the inspirations given by Job's soul. Job's temptation was to conclude on the basis of outer misfortune that the God of the ego had turned his back on him, and that he should escape from his troubles by renouncing Jehovah.

Where Elias is concerned we see the opposite interpretation of suffering. Just when all the outer circumstances are very difficult, when the hindrances are strong, there is the best opportunity to exercise the strength of one's ego. Rudolf Steiner goes on to say:

> The period we are looking at now is a similar time of distress, a period of famine. And many a person had turned away from Jehovah because they could no longer trust the way he was behaving when they saw how he treated the people during the terrible famine. If it is possible to speak of progress with regard to the Jehovah principle, we shall have to characterize this progress in the following way. A divine principle needed to appear which, although it was the same Jehovah principle as of old, was to be filled with greater human understanding to the point where it could be said: Whatever may occur in the outer world, however happy a person's life may be, or however afflicted he is by misery and distress,

these external things are in no way a proof of the benevolence or the wrath of Jehovah. No. A person has the right approach, the right respect for the Jehovah principle, if he does not waver in his devotion to the invisible God, however great his distress and misery, and is filled with the certainty: He is! not through any external observations, but solely on the basis of the forces of his own soul. This change of attitude needed to come about at that time.

Here we see Elias' mission providing the actual solution to the Job riddle. It demonstrates that each human being is called upon to work on his ego forces, the Jehovah forces, making them ever deeper and more individual. This leads to the opposite interpretation of the function of the whole external environment. It does not exist in order to carry the human being, which is the case when all is well. Neither does it exist so that a human being can identify with it and merge into it. From now on the task of outer existence is rather to offer the human ego the right challenge, the right resistance.

Elias' life makes Elias the forerunner of the Ego Being who incarnated at the turning-point of time into the depths of the individual human being. Through the appearance of Elias the thought arises in humankind: As a human individuality a person can, even before his birth, choose very difficult karmic circumstances, and see them not as a punishment, not as the consequence of accrued guilt, nor as a sign of being deserted by Jehovah, but just the reverse. He wants to increase his ego forces to overcome all hindrances and difficulties. No ego development is possible without suffering and struggle.

Thus the mystery of Elias clearly points to the further individualization of human beings in the course of coming to terms with the suffering and all the difficulties which confront us as our positive karmic task.

Individualism as Universalism

As the final result of the evolution of the Jewish people the appearance of Elias proclaims the mystery of the individual ego, the eternal individuality in every human being, which develops ever further from one incarnation to another. The good part of life is not that everything goes well in a superficial way, but that the godlike force of the ego comes to expression in each human being in an ever purer, more spiritual, more individual way.

To sum up, we can present the pattern of the evolution of the Jewish people right up to the fulfilment, to the turning-point of time, by looking at the three main stages: the *Abraham stage* as the bodily formation that was destined in course of time to be given to the whole of humankind as a basis for the ego activity of each human being; the *Moses stage* as the addition of the right inward-ness of soul, the right activation of the human self as a soul preparation for ego-nature, for the purely spiritual ele-ment; and the *Elias impulse* presenting a significant pointer to the completing of this by the spirit of the individual ego (this is why Elias returns as John the Baptist, who points to the Sun Being as the final fulfilment of the mission of the Jewish people).

If we grasp the mission of Elias in such a way that we experience the bodily basis, the blood of the people, and the soul basis, their faith in the law, as a twofold condition for a third factor, then we understand the *humanly universal* mission of the Jewish people.

So long as the exercising of the ego was determined by the forces of the blood and the submission to the law, their evolution had a preparatory character. Both aspects — the bodily and the soul dimensions — fulfil their significance in that they prepare the way for the third aspect: the totally *individual quality* and spiritual dimension of ego activity.

At this third stage it is no longer a decisive issue which

nation or people a human being belongs to. In the perspective of reincarnation *every human being* has, in the
course of pre-Christian times, been through the evolution
presented in the history of the Jewish people. Each one of us
has taken part in some form in the body and soul stage of
the ego evolution of Judaism. This means that the ability to
pass through the Elias stage to the point of becoming an
individual is potentially there in everybody. This is where
the inherent *universalism* of the Jewish principle lies. Its very
nature is to lead to the individual ego, which at one and the
same time *each and every* human being has in common with
all the others.

Therefore the message of the prophet Elias can be summarized as follows. The crucial factor in the Jehovah principle actually does not consist in support by a group (nation
or law) or in the smiling prosperity of outer events. Quite
the reverse: it lies in the nature of ego activity whereby each
human being acquires the experience of individual spiritual
autonomy, and achieves this in the face of every sort of
outer resistance.

For the Hebraic people the promise above all other
promises was the coming of the Messiah. It is the focus and
the meaning of Jewish religion. To this day the Jewish
people are still awaiting his coming, and the ways in which
they imagine this happening are manifold. But there is one
thing they all have in common: his arrival will bear the
character of fulfilment and finality. This finality, however,
also applies to the power of the ego Elias calls upon, for this
is of a purely inner, spiritual and individual nature, and
resists any identification with anything either external or of
a group nature. However, it lay in the nature of the mission
of the Jewish people to bring the individual to the point of
overcoming all identification with national traits.

Even if Jehovah is initially understood to be a national
God he nevertheless works to prepare for and make
possible the *character* of finality: the exercising of pure

individuality and, arising out of it, pure *universality*. As the *national* God he has to be at the service of the universally human principle.

Expectation of the Messiah or Fulfilment of the Law?

Now the question arises: if the working of Jehovah had been experienced *before Elias* in the forces of the blood and in the observance of the law of the people, where does the *absolutely new*, individual force come from which Elias experiences and proclaims as being beyond the blood and the law, so that a 'righteous person' with his loyalty to Jehovah can suffer even more than other people?

The central question, when discussing Judaism and Christianity, was and is: do we still live today in a time of expectation — the expectation of the advent of the Messiah — or do we live in a time of fulfilment?

Traditional Christianity has answered this question in the following way. The Messiah — 'Christos' is the Greek translation of the Hebraic *Meschiach*, the Annointed One — has already come, he is here, and we have been living for the past two thousand years in the time of accomplishment and fulfilment.

Traditional Judaism has given the opposite answer. The Messiah has not yet come — when he comes the course of things will not only be accomplished but time will *come to an end*; what the Christians call 'Christ' cannot possibly be regarded as the Jewish Messiah.

Rudolf Steiner's spiritual science sees both these basic conceptions as right and both of them also as one-sided. Each one needs to be complemented by the other, in order to encompass the whole of reality.

In support of the basic tenets of traditional Christianity: since the Mystery of Golgotha the all-embracing cosmic Being of Love permeates the entire spectrum of the earth's forces, creating the final—total and complete—conditions for all the further evolution of every member of human-kind. Through his activity he makes possible the exercising of the individual, spiritually creative ego, which cannot be replaced by any *essentially* higher stage.

Whether this uniqueness of ego activity—even if only rudimentary to start with—is actually possible or not can-not be decided by abstract speculation. Freedom is a reality; it cannot be proved but only produced. There have actually been people—such as Goethe—who have practised it to a high degree. It can be deduced from this that the forces of human uniqueness *actually do exist* and are at everyone's actual disposal.

But up to now traditional Christianity has been one-sided, especially where its opposition to Judaism is concerned. For the coming of the Messiah—of the Christ—to humanity, does not have only one but two basic dimensions. The one is the substance of the Christ's Being, what he achieves and what he thereby enables every human being to do. The other no less important aspect of his 'coming' is the way in which he makes his entry, spiritually, into the inner being of each human individual. This depends on the individual freedom of each one of us.

For this gradual 'entry' of the Christ into the human individual the *whole of the second half* of evolution is required. In this respect each human being is still right at the beginning of the process of getting to know the Christ principle and making it his own. In this second sense the basic tenet of Judaism is more applicable than the tra-ditional Christian one: the Messiah is still coming; his actual entry into each human individual lies in the future far more than in the past.

The anti-Jewish one-sidedness of traditional Christianity is to a large extent due to the fact that the Christ event is seen far too little as the actual evolutionary perspective of each human ego. And the reason for this is due not least to the fact that the consciousness of reincarnation has been lost. The Christianity of 'faith' pins its hopes on receiving everything from the Christ in one single life, because it still expects everything to happen by divine 'Grace'.

The future of Christianity can only lie in the fact that the individual human being regards the advent of the Christ Being in his ego, the Christianizing of his ego, as the *future* coming of the Messiah, as the still outstanding task of human freedom. In this respect the 'Christian' can fully agree with the 'Jew'.

The antichristian one-sidedness of traditional Judaism consisted in not sufficiently recognizing the character of achievement that has governed the life of humankind for some time now. The Sun Being of Love—the Messiah—has already 'visited' the earth and made it into his body. The 'fullness of time', the fulfilment of evolution, is already there in the sense that all the essential requirements for the rest of human evolution are already actually available. The quality of completion lies in the fact that it is now actually possible to exercise and experience individual ego nature and the universal quality of being human. This experience will become possible through seeing and experiencing as a *preparatory stage* everything that is of a group nature—either on a bodily level or on a soul/cultural level—and experiencing this preparatory stage as the foundation and prerequisite upon which human individuality and human universality can and should arise.

Up till now traditional Christianity has been less a Christianity of the spirit than of the soul, that is, of a group nature. This explains the central role of the Church. People lived, moreover, largely according to the 'law'—only to think of the role of canonical law and the Inquisition. The inner freedom and spiritual autonomy of the single individual was in fact often regarded as 'antichristian', as a sin. Real Christianity too—just like the Messiah—is still wholly in the process of coming!

Through Rudolf Steiner's spiritual science a completely new level of 'tolerance' can arise among the religions. Judaism can open itself to the Christian principle if it actually starts acquiring the absolute uniqueness of individualism and universalism. Christianity can open itself to the Jewish principle by finding in the exercise of human freedom, which is still in its beginning stages, the actual fulfilment of divine Grace.

The 'Wandering Jew' and the 'Eternally Traditional Christian'

In the medieval legend of Ahasuerus, the Wandering Jew, we can find deep secrets expressed in the form of images. Ahasuerus is a Jew, and yet not only a Jew. He appears again in Goethe's writings, not as a Jew but as the image of the evolution of Everyman. What kind of person is it who remains a 'Jew' forever? He is *Everyman* in so far as he is still confined to a group, even after the coming of the Christ, and does not find his way to becoming universally human through the further development of his own individual ego.

He is entirely given up to one particular principle of one particular nation, culture or religion, and misses out on the decisive 'turning-point' of evolution by not turning away from the exclusiveness of any one-sided principle in order to turn to the entirety and synthesis of human nature in its wholeness.

In the legend of the Wandering or Eternal Jew we see the struggle going on within Christianity for self-understanding and for individual identity. The deeper, really *Christian* meaning of this legend is that Ahasuerus is every Christian who thinks of himself as already 'redeemed' and as belonging from the outset to the host—the group!—of the chosen ones. The Wandering Jew is every Christian who never *becomes* a real human being because he identifies himself with what he has been given through the blood and the Church. Because he thinks he is already a Christian he cannot become one. He understands Grace not as a challenge to each human being to become free but as a possession and a privilege — as a distinguishing mark that makes him better than other people.

On the one hand Ahasuerus — Everyman — feels an irresistible attraction to the Representative of Humanity who holds his hand out to him. He would like to take his hand, but he nevertheless feels the urge to take evasive action and resist him. This picture expresses the perpetual conflict taking place in every human being between his higher and his lower ego.

The lower ego wants the comfort and automatisms arising from being swallowed up by the qualities of his bodily nature and of a group-soul nature. The force of attraction that Ahasuerus experiences as coming to him from the hand of Christ is a picture of the fact that every human being in his true, higher ego has the potential and the call to become both individual and universal, to become in fact truly human.

The Joint Karma of the Jewish and the German People

Perhaps you will permit me to conclude these thoughts about the mission of the Jewish people with a reference to the special karma that connects the Jewish people with the German people. As recently as this century we have seen that in the whole history of humankind there have hardly been two peoples so deeply and tragically intertwined as the Germans and the Jews. The karma which these two peoples have mutually prepared for themselves is so enormous that there is a very great call to understand this mystery in greater and greater depth. In the mutual karma of these two peoples a great deal is concealed which is quite simply a part of the evolution of the whole of humankind.

If we base it on Rudolf Steiner's spiritual science, previously undreamed of perspectives arise to help us approach this mystery. One can say: the mission of the Jewish people was quite simply to prepare and to make possible the coming of the Messiah, the dawning of true human nature. For this to happen a suitable body and a suitable soul had to be provided.

This is saying that it was the special mission of the Jewish people to awaken in humanity a consciousness of the fact that everything which needed preparing in isolation—on an 'exclusive' level—was destined to become later on the common possession of the whole of humankind. The Jewish people had the mission to understand that any 'exclusiveness' is not a privilege but a moral responsibility to the whole of humankind, a duty and a service. In this sense any 'exclusiveness' cannot but be of a temporary nature.

The fulfilling of the mission of Judaism consists in finding the sacrificial forces to overcome any claim to exclusiveness and to understand the universal obligation of their own mission. True Judaism is fulfilled in *universalism* of an all-embracing, human character.

In the German people we have all the cultural prerequisites for the polar opposite impulse. In German classicism, especially in Goetheanism and idealism, there arises for the first time in history human *individualism* in the best sense of the word. We have only to think of the philosophy of Fichte.

These two fundamental impulses—universalism and individualism—relate to one another like the activity of the Son and the Holy Spirit in humankind. In both cases a 'chosen people' has, during the period of preparation, acted as agent for the whole of humankind.

At the beginning of the twentieth century Rudolf Steiner's spiritual science, an impulse essentially connected to the working of the Holy Spirit, was introduced to humankind in Middle Europe, along a path that connected it intimately with the karma of the German people. This great event in the domain of consciousness can be seen as a kind of sending of the Holy Spirit on the part of Christ. A significant task of spiritual science is the reconciliation of Judaism and Christianity.

To the extent that these two peoples fail to fulfil their mission there will be a corresponding lack of true universalism and free individualism in humankind. The failure of these two peoples is a failure on the part of the whole of humanity. The vast human tragedy of this failure will inevitably fall back on these two peoples. The twentieth century has shown us this in the most shattering way.

Evolution, however, is not yet finished. The whole of humankind awaits the time when the insistence on a preoccupation with blood and soil will be transformed into universal love and individual freedom in the heart of every man and woman on earth.

5
THE TURNING-POINT OF TIME —
THEN AND ALWAYS

The mission of Judaism can be summed up in its culminating task of preparing the right bodily sheaths destined to receive—in the thirtieth year of the life of Jesus of Nazareth—the incarnation of the central Being of our solar system. Human nature and the human bodily sheaths—affected in the way they were by the Fall—were, in the course of the generations of the Jewish people, so purified and ennobled that they were made capable of receiving the World Logos, the Cosmic Word.

The turning-point of time consists in the fact that the Being of Love, who in the primeval stage of evolution drew forth the sun as a heavenly body from the earth, is now, through his incarnation, through his entry into the earth forces in their entirety, introducing a gradual reunion of the earth and the sun and therefore also of the planets belonging to the solar system.

We can repeat the question afresh: what is the meaning of the fact that in the beginnings of evolution the sun withdrew from the earth? In his *Occult Science: an Outline*, Rudolf Steiner describes it in this way. In the primal beginning the necessity occurred for the Being of Love to withdraw from the entire complex of earth forces. The departure of the Sun Being from the earth can be seen as belonging to the whole complex of the Fall.

Through the fact of the Sun Being distancing himself from the body of the earth, the other being who is called Lucifer was given the opportunity to govern the first half of evolution which portrays the negative phase of freedom. Through the Fall there began the evolution of egoism, the separating and splitting up of human beings. For indivi-dualization and freedom are possible only if they are preceded by a first negative phase of separation, of dismissal.

This is repeated again on a small scale in every human life. After the first paradisaic phase of identifying with their parents children experience the negative phase of freedom. In order to find their own identity and achieve indepen-dence children have to draw away and distance themselves from everybody. This again can be likened to the already mentioned departure of the Prodigal Son from his father's home in the Gospel parable.

The Freedom of Egoism and the Freedom of Love

Knowing that the negative phase of freedom was essential for evolution — the phase which was originally activated by the basic principle of egoism — the Being of Love allowed this to come about by withdrawing from the body of the earth. He made way for the necessary activity of egoism, for Lucifer.

The second, positive phase of freedom begins when human beings start overcoming egoism through the forces of love. This is what makes them truly free. The freedom of egoism, the freedom to oppose others and to do as one wants at all costs, not knowing what we are doing to one another, is actually only the beginning of freedom, only the imperfect stage of freedom.

The phase of perfect freedom begins for human beings when a conscious and deliberate effort is made to overcome egoism through the forces of love. The self-same forces a person acquired by taking possession of the whole world in an egoistic way have now to flow back in service to the total organism of humanity.

Love enables a human being to understand that separate

existence is only an illusion, and that the spirit which unites all human beings consists in the fact that each single human being is a member of the whole organism of humankind. Humankind is in the real sense a single spiritual organism. It is absolutely impossible that one human being could achieve happiness and perfection without the happiness and perfection of everyone.

Therefore we understand that the fulness of time and the turning of the times consists in the Being of Love returning to the earth now that this first phase of development under the sway of egoism has been absolved. This event happened gradually and was prophesied by the initiates in the Mysteries. Through the fact that the Sun Being as a spiritual entity finally and conclusively withdrew from the body of the sun two thousand years ago to make the earth into his body, sun and earth – as planetary bodies – have been for two thousand years in the process of coming closer to one another in order to become a single planetary body again in the course of ages. This will bring it about that the other planets of the solar system also become a unity again.

Jesus of Nazareth and the Fulfilment of the Law

Out of the whole of humankind the Jewish people were the only people capable of preparing a suitable bodily vessel for the incarnation of the Logos. The Christ Being could incarnate only among the Jewish people. This is the particular mystery of Jesus of Nazareth as the person destined to become the Christ Bearer. His body contained all the human characteristics inscribed in the bodily nature of the Hebrew people throughout their history. The meaning and fulfilment of everything that happened in the history of the Jewish people was the creation of this one body and the birth of Jesus of Nazareth as the future bearer of the Messiah.

Jesus of Nazareth offered the Christ Being the only body suitable at that time in the whole of humanity to receive the Logos, the body which was the best adapted and the most willing to receive it. Further, this enabled the Sun Being to incarnate into the three bodily sheaths at the age of 30. The baptism in the Jordan is the actual entry of the Sun Being, the Being of Love, into the threefold bodily nature of the human being prepared throughout the whole evolution of the Jewish people.

It was through the incarnation of the cosmic Word that the fulfilment of the law and the fullness of time came to be. The return of the Sun Being to the earth brings to completion all the conditions necessary for the second half of evolution, for the evolution of the forces of Love.

If we look again at the three fundamental phases in the evolution of the Hebrew people we can say that at the *Abraham* stage a bodily basis was created on the strength of which each single human being could attain individualization; at the *Moses* stage the human soul was given the capacity to internalize the law and the meaning of evolution; and through *Elias* this evolution is deepened in the direction of the spirit, in that the individual mystery of karma, particularly when the blows of destiny are particularly painful, is not regarded as a sin or as a punishment but as an evolutionary opportunity bearing an entirely individual character.

This threefold path has been traversed by each one of us, for it represents the three stages of all human development. Each of us bears within ourselves as a result of our total evolution the bodily nature of Abraham, the laws of Moses and the individuality of Elias. This has to become more and more conscious and real.

This is how we have to understand the *fulfilment of the law*. It consists in the fact that the human being fulfils and consummates the 'law', meaning the purpose and plan of evolution, by producing from out of himself more and more ego strength, more and more of a feeling of responsibilty for creation and an ability to take his own part in it.

In this sense Paul is right when he says: It is not sin that has produced the law, but the law sin. This to be understood as saying that it was in the very nature of the law of evolution that a separation, an atomizing of humanity had to come about, so that ego-nature could arise at all. This separation, this 'Fall into sin' should be understood to begin with not in a moral sense, not as something evil, but as a primal necessity of evolution, as the prerequisite altogether of becoming a morally free and responsible individual.

The coming of the Sun Being to the earth and to humankind fulfils the law of evolution, and paves the way for the law of ego development to be accomplished.

I and the Father (Father Abraham) are One

In St John's Gospel the mysteries of the Logos, the mysteries of the whole meaning of evolution are presented in a particularly profound way. In the long conflict-laden arguments between the Christ Being and the scribes and Pharisees they are constantly discussing the correct meaning of the law of Moses. The Christ is blamed for contradicting and disregarding the law, whereas he repeatedly points out that, quite on the contrary, he is working to bring about the fulfilment of the law in the sense that through him the law will have attained its purpose.

For instance, in the eighth to the tenth chapter of the St John's Gospel we see a certain culmination of the first part up to the raising of Lazarus. In the eighth chapter the interpretation of the *Abraham stage* is presented as the very kernel of the argument. The key statement, which describes the way a Jew of those times experienced himself, is: We are children of Abraham, we are the seed of Abraham. This is saying, our identity lies in our body, in our blood. We bear the kind of body in which the spirit of Jehovah works. Only people with the bodily nature of Abraham can say of themselves that they are filled with the spirit of Jehovah.

The scribes and Pharisees see the fact of their belonging to this folk spirit and this ancestral blood as a mark of distinction, as a privilege in the sense that not all people but only those belonging to this particular nation can claim this important connection with the Godhead. Everyone else is excluded. This statement, which sums up the self-understanding and self-awareness of a Jew of those times, is countered by Christ with the words: 'Before Abraham was, there was the I AM.' This is usually translated as 'Before Abraham was, I was.' But Christ is saying that the being of the ego was there before Abraham, which means that the bodily nature of Abraham possessed by the Jews is a partial aspect of the overall plan of evolution. This consists in ego-nature becoming possible and also being realized through the human being and in all human beings.

The first thing that has to be there, even before the partial aspects and the intermediary steps can be considered, is always the overall plan and the meaning and goal of the whole of evolution. Before the role played by Abraham could even have been considered the overall plan had to be established: 'Before Abraham was, was the I AM.' The arising of the experience of the 'I am' is the whole meaning of it all. The single contributions are formed accordingly and are subordinate.

The Jews said: 'I and Father Abraham are one.' This was how they identified themselves for the time being with this particular and partial aspect of evolution. Christ counters this with a statement which deliberately omits the word 'Abraham': 'I and the Father are one.' Ego-nature is experienced in a unity with the universal *spiritual* Father of all humankind. 'I and the Father are one.'

The very character of consummation, of the fullness of time, consists in human beings beginning to identify with the whole, with universality, with the Father of all of us. This spiritual Father does not only give us a physical body – like Abraham – but wants each one of us to become his son as an ego-endowed co-creator.

Moses Spoke of the Mysteries of the Ego

In the following ninth chapter the kernel of the argument is now the other statement of the scribes: 'We are disciples of Moses.' Now they are not only talking of Abraham's bodily nature but of the body of the law. 'We are disciples of Moses' means: 'Our identity, the contents of our souls are the commandments of Moses, the Torah, the law. Obeying the law gives us our self-esteem. We experience our humanity in that we have the law of Moses in common.'

Christ countered this statement by saying: 'Moses wrote of the I AM.' The usual translation is: 'Moses wrote of me' (John 5:46). This statement in the St John's Gospel is not easily understood by many theologians. They wonder where Moses writes about the Christ. We have already seen what the essence of Moses' Ten Commandments is: they are the laws of becoming an ego. Moses was all the time writing about the nature of the ego.

In the tenth chapter we have then the final consequence of this intensification. First statement: 'We are children of Abraham.' First counter-statement: 'Before Abraham was, was the I AM.' Second statement: 'We are disciples of Moses.' Second counter-statement: 'Moses spoke of the I AM.' The final consequence of this fulfilment of the law through ego development is expressed in the powerful statement in chapter ten: 'Ye are gods! [υεοι έστε].' Here, too, Christ is quoting the Old Testament! Each human being bears within himself the actual capacity to become more and more godlike, to become an ever more spiritually independent being, a divine sovereign being. Through experiencing himself, in the activation of his own thinking in a more and more intuitive and individual way, as a spiritual being in a purely spiritual world, the human being will take an ever more active share in God's creative powers.

We see in what way the fulfilment of time and the consummation of the law as the very law of evolution takes place through the Christ event. This happens through the overcoming of every partial impulse and identification in a particular group. The Being of Love leads on the one hand to a universalism that encompasses the whole of humankind, and on the other hand to complete individualization of each person.

Stoning the Adulteress to Death?

In the eighth chapter of St John's Gospel there is a description of the scene with the adulteress. It is an event that combines so many things, represents the prototype of so much, that we can regard this scene with the adulteress as an archetypal phenomenon of the transition from separate existence to the fullness and fulfilment of the whole, where the universally human factor is called upon.

What is being narrated here must also be taken absolutely seriously from a historical point of view. It is, in the first place, a historical happening. It must be accepted according to the facts it describes. A woman is taken in adultery. Yet, as we have indicated, it is also a picture encapsulating the whole course of evolution.

They bring the woman to Christ with the question: 'What sayest thou? The law of Moses says we should stone to death any woman caught in adultery. What dost *thou* say?' Christ stoops down and writes on the ground. And when they appeal to him again he makes the statement: 'He that is without sin among you, let him first cast a stone at her.'

We may well ask the question whether the law of Moses in any case means that a woman caught in adultery ought to be physically put to death by stoning. For if the law of Moses is meant to be a loving and beneficial law one wonders what is achieved by stoning such a person to death.

Therefore Christ says: He that is without sin among you let him first cast a stone. And they all go away, beginning with the eldest, who had had more time to sin. Remaining alone with the woman Christ asks her: Has no one condemned thee? And she says, no one. And he said, neither do I condemn thee. Continue to develop (which is usually translated as 'go'!) and sin no more.

We encounter here a colossal misunderstanding of the law of Moses, which explains why the fulfilment of this law was also misunderstood at the time. For Moses cannot possibly have meant people to stone such a person to death. This would serve the sole purpose of depriving the person of further development, when there is the greatest need of it. The meaning of Moses' law must certainly be quite different. If we understand the spirit of Moses' law aright we must give an entirely different interpretation to this passage of the Old Testament.

The Jewish people are told: As distinct from other people, you have to develop the impulse of the ego, the impulse of liberating human beings from natural necessity. You must become more and more conscious of this sense for human evolution. For you, natural necessity should solely be a basis for what can be further built on it, namely, human ego development in the spirit of freedom. This evolutionary law pointing to the ego is given you in the law of Moses.

If you understand the meaning of this law properly you will also understanding the following. A person who is all wrapped up in his own drives, in the natural part of himself – in the law of nature, which also comes to expression in his bodily drives and instincts, and strongest of all in sexual desire – is not yet fully human. You must understand the law of Moses in such a way that you are convinced that a human being who does not add to his natural part the ego element and the element of freedom is as regards his humanity still dead. You will only understand the evolutionary law of Moses properly and will only have the right idea of a human being when you learn to think of an entirely instinctive human being as being dead. Where your thinking is concerned, a person who is entirely on the level of nature counts as dead. Now where do you see an image of extreme natural necessity? In the mineral kingdom, in the realm of the stones. So if you have the right thoughts about the meaning and goal of the law of evolution revealed to you through Moses you will think of a purely instinctive person as being *dead as a stone*. In your thinking you will consider that person, from the human point of view, just as dead as a stone, because a person of that kind has fallen back to the mineral stage. He is as much a part of nature as a stone is, and there is as yet nothing human or free about him — as a human being he is dead.

This can be the only meaning that God intended the law of Moses to have. There is no question of any other interpretation. In the course of the evolution of the Jewish people, however, its meaning has been thoroughly misunderstood. This misunderstanding itself belongs, on the other hand, to the evolution of the whole of humankind. Because of increasing materialism a spiritual content was interpreted in a purely physical/material way. So that already in Christ's time the following interpretation predominated: if a woman is caught in adultery she should be physically stoned to death with physical stones. If the whole thing was meant on a *physical* level, however, one ought to raise the question: and what of the man? Why should he not be stoned? It takes two people to commit adultery.

So the scribes and Pharisees cannot continue to hold this interpretation with an entirely clear conscience. This is seen in the fact that on the one hand they had hoped Christ would declare their action legitimate or, on the other hand they had thought he might not approve of this killing. Thus they evince great doubt in their own way of interpreting the law.

The Human Soul as Cosmic Adulteress

We can regard the picture shown here in a historical event as an *archetypal phenomenon* of the evolution of humankind and thereby considerably broaden the perspectives of our interpretation.

The act of adultery which has occurred in the karma of this woman is an image of the actual evolution of every human being, an image of the law of evolution altogether.

In the course of evolution the human soul was, in the earliest beginnings, wedded to its first husband, the spirit. This first wedding, this initial marriage to the cosmic spirit, had to come to an end. To bring the meaning and purpose of evolution to any kind of realization the human soul had to separate from the spirit, had to become 'unfaithful' to the spirit. This 'infidelity' is not wicked in a moral sense, as has been frequently indicated, but an evolutionary necessity. The human soul had to leave behind it its initial attachment to and its feeling of being at home in the spiritual cosmos. It had to unite with the second husband with whom it can form a union in the course of evolution: with the body, the bodily element of the cosmos.

The adultery scene in the St John's Gospel is a historical happening as well as a comprehensive parable of evolution. The adulteress is also every human soul. In Holy Scripture every female figure is an image of the soul and its qualities.

To enable individualization and egohood to come about at all the human soul had to leave its first husband, the spirit, so that it might unite with its second husband, the bodily element of earth. We must not frown in a moral sense upon this adultery or, as we have already said, endeavour to revoke it. Human beings should not return to the state they were in at the beginning. This would thwart the whole point of evolution, and it would have happened in vain.

Evolution should not continue in a backward direction but forwards. The fact that this adultery can be regarded, with respect to further evolution, as having a positive significance is demonstrated by Christ in not condemning the adulteress—the human soul. He writes the full evolutionary fact of the adultery in the earth. He writes the necessities of the evolution of a human being on his own earth body, for the earth has to become the scene and the place of every human being's evolutionary possibilities.

The human soul has united itself with the body of the earth by breaking faith with the spirit. The Being of Love is uniting himself with the body of the earth to accompany the human soul in its body-bound evolution.

The call to the human soul to develop further and to sin no more means: you are going to revoke the separation from the spirit—the necessary 'sin' of evolution, but not in the sense that you return to your original state. You should *develop further* (πο-ρευου, the usual translation of which is 'go', and which does not tell us anything).

You shall further strengthen and purify your individuality through the forces of your own ego and the practice of freedom, so that you can connect once more with the spirit but now in freedom, which is the true meaning of the word *religion*. This means bringing the goal of evolution to realization.

Christianity is the Religion of the Earth

The essence of the Christ event is that the cosmic Being of Love is uniting himself with the sum total of the earth's forces and is filling and transforming it with his Love so powerfully that our 'redemption' is being made possible.

Because of the Fall, because of the cosmic adultery of falling into the earthly element of separation – into the physical/material bodily sheaths – the human soul has become too closely akin to the body. Human beings experienced more and more their own impotence of soul in the face of natural necessity.

The Mystery of Golgotha, the mystical deed of the Being of Love, is an all-round empowerment of the human being, giving each one of us the ability to experience and strengthen the actual soul's force of attraction towards the spirit. Through the 'redemption' the soul is given back its 'affinity to the spirit'. To cultivate this tension with regard to the spirit, to practise it until it becomes more and more real – Aristotle and Thomas Aquinas would say to transform it from potentiality to actuality – is the never-ending task of human freedom.

Christ writes the human act of 'adultery' into the body of the earth, and Christianity is the religion of the earth. Human beings cannot be redeemed by forsaking matter. By doing so they would only be committing 'adultery' for a second time – after having been unfaithful to the spirit they would then become unfaithful to the earth. They would be forsaking the place of all future evolution.

Through writing in the earth Christ is telling every human being: you will return to the earth again and again until the earth has also become a part of the redemption. The world of matter became mineral *for your sake* to make your individualization possible. The whole *mineral kingdom* came into being for your sake. Your union with the realm of the stones is not there in order to 'stone to death' your humanity. But neither do the stones want to be ungratefully forsaken by you and left behind. They want to resurrect *within you* in that in the course of future evolution you *transform* them into the substance of your own spirit.

Christianity is the religion of transformation — of transsubstantiation — of everything material into human spirit. All
creation is yearning to become human.

When the evolutionary impulse that has up till now been
given the name of 'Christianity' has been properly understood, it cannot be regarded as one religion *alongside* others.
This has been indicated many times. The human individuality who, in his thirtieth year, laid at the disposal of the
Christ Being his threefold bodily instrument — the physical
body, the body of life forces and the soul sheath — cannot be
regarded as the 'founder of a new religion'.

Jesus and the Christ: Human Expectation and Divine Fulfilment

The name 'Jesus Christ' points to a twofold element. 'Jesus'
is the human being who becomes the Christ bearer. 'Christ'
is the divine cosmic Word which unites with this human
vessel to use it as an instrument and in the course of the
three years of the Incarnation to enter fully into it.

Thus we can say: in Jesus of Nazareth we have a summing up, in one individual, of all human religious practice
in its need and longing for redemption. He was the *religion
of the whole of humanity* actualized and made one. We can
experience the essence of humanity in such an archetypal
and representative manner within one individual that we
should not speak of a human being at all but of *the* human
being.

What actually took place in Jesus of Nazareth's thirtieth
year is something that no religion before Christ could speak
about, because this occurrence had never taken place
before. What was prophesied by initiates of all religions as a
future event — that the exalted Sun Being would come to the
earth to gradually transform the earth into a sun again —
became reality in the Mystery of Golgotha.

What was happening was not the founding of any kind of new religion. It was an event that brought 'redemption' to the whole of humanity. It was not the deed of a human founder of religion – however highly developed we might consider him to be. It was the incarnation of the central spiritual Being of the solar system, comprising all the forces of cosmic Love, so that he could pour them into the earth to enable every human being to be free. The Christ event has to do directly with each and every human being. Every aspect of this event was on a scale that combined both the cosmos and humanity, therefore our attitude to it can be formed only on a purely individual basis. Jesus of Nazareth represented personally the moral/religious conscience of the whole of humanity through bringing to consciousness the necessity for redemption.

It is not easy to speak of the Being of Love, of the divine Sun Being, because over the past two thousand years, where traditional Christianity is concerned, the *cosmic* dimension of the Christ event has been lost sight of. Our way of looking at it has become more and more restricted to the *human* dimension. The divine part of his Being was understood less and less.

In the earliest centuries after the coming of Christ there still existed the last traces of the ancient Gnosis. This fading knowledge enabled some people to have a faint glimmer of the cosmic and divine character of the Mystery of Golgotha. This Gnosis, even the last traces of this ancient wisdom, had totally disappeared by the fourth century after Christ. In the centuries after the age of Constantine there was hardly any chance any more for humanity to grasp the cosmic significance of the Christ Mystery. The interpretation of this Mystery came increasingly down to the 'human' level, until in the end people could see only 'the simple man of Nazareth'.

Christianity as a Mystical and Cosmic Fact

Rudolf Steiner's fundamental statement regarding Christianity is the following: Real, genuine Christianity does not begin to take root in humankind until human beings realize that they are no longer dealing with one religion among other religions, but that so-called 'Christianity' represents the fulfilment of all the religions. In this sense it is also the overcoming of 'religion' as such, as a specific pre-Christian phenomenon.

The essence of religion prior to Christ's coming—in fact of every 'religion'—is to be seen in the human efforts to foster a contact with the Godhead. Religious practices— whether prayer or ritual or anything else—are human deeds. Even theology is something that lives in human beings as wisdom or treasures of knowledge about the Godhead, even if its origin lies in divine revelation.

True Christianity, however, is not in the first place a human religion but—as Rudolf Steiner claims—primarily an 'affair of the gods'. The spiritual Hierarchies, from the angels right up to the Seraphim, had been faced for long ages with an insoluble riddle. What human beings called 'death' was totally unknown to them. And yet human beings complained to them more and more bitterly of suffering and death.

Therefore in a council of all the divine hierarchical beings they reached the resolution to send down to the earth the Sun Spirit as their loving representative, in order to experience human death. Together with them and out of love for them the Being of Love resolved to become a human being, so as to be able to experience for himself what every human being experiences when he passes through death—both at the end of life and in the many forms of dying that take place daily.

So all the angelic beings waited with bated breath as the blood flowed on Golgotha and the Sun Spirit left the body.

Throughout the cosmos they were awaiting with the greatest eagerness: What will HE tell us about human death? Will he also complain about it and call it a threat to existence altogether, as human beings do when they think 'dying' means ceasing to exist?. . . How can human beings possibly imagine the *cosmic rejoicing* experienced in heaven when on Easter Sunday the Christ brought to all the heavenly beings the tidings that there is *no such thing* as death! Human beings are afraid of something that does not exist. What they call 'death' is in reality only the fear of not being able to continue existing as purely spiritual beings as *we* do. The Fall into sin is human consciousness falling into the illusion of death. Human *consciousness* has to be redeemed. Death is only a phenomenon within human consciousness. . .

In what *way* it became possible for the Sun Being, as a divine Being, actually to experience human death for himself is one of the profoundest and most complicated mysteries that exist. Rudolf Steiner's spiritual science in particular has a great deal to contribute to a gradual disclosing of this mystery. In this instance, too, a *Being of a soul nature* had to mediate and make possible the uniting of a purely spiritual Being – the Christ – with the bodily element.

Rudolf Steiner describes that before the Mystery of Golgotha there came about on three occasions, through the mediation of soul substance that was part of humanity, i.e. the twin soul of Adam who had remained in innocence in Paradise, a union of the Sun Being with humankind. The future Nathan soul of the St Luke Gospel functioned at that time as the soul of an archangel, with the ability to feel endless compassion for suffering humanity. The Sun Being was able to enter into this soul being three times, even if not yet directly into a physical body as in the Mystery of Golgotha. On the first occasion it was the senses that were 'redeemed', i.e. restored to a condition worthy of humankind; on the second occasion it was the vital organs; and the third time it was the soul forces. On the fourth occasion, at the Mystery of Golgotha, the ego forces were to be harmonized. Through the mediation of the soul of an archangelic being, the Sun Being was able each time to feel compassion for our human condition.

Also on the fourth occasion, the Mystery of Golgotha, it was again through the mediation of a soul being that the Christ was enabled actually to experience for himself, for example, the fear every human being has to experience at death.

The 'Ascension' and the Threefold 'Descent into Hell'

The experience of death was a decisive part of Christ's incarnation. The inhabiting of a body is only experienced fully when death is experienced.

Speaking of 'death' only has a meaning to the extent that the person neglects to develop an element that cannot die. If the human being makes an effort, however, to strengthen in himself and make more and more real the eternal core of his being that passes from incarnation to incarnation and knows no death, if he makes an effort to develop an independent individuality, a real spiritual ego nature, death cannot harm him.

This 'immortality', however, as already mentioned, is not an automatic matter, but a question of individual development. So it is up to each human being to work on *acquiring* a more and more real immortality for himself.

The cosmic dimension of the Christ event is expressed in what is called the 'Descent into Hell' and the 'Ascension'. A consciousness such as Christ has is the highest possible 'heaven' in our cycle of evolution. The Christ himself is the real heaven. There is no other heaven. He tells each human being that by making the earth into his body he is with us until the end of earth days. Thus the Christ is united with the earth and will be found on the earth throughout the second half of evolution. The so-called Ascension of Christ is not to be understood in the sense that Christ went away and deserted the earth. On the contrary, Christ founded heaven on earth. He himself is becoming the earth's and humanity's real heaven. Through the fact that by means of his spiritual presence he is making the body of the earth into a place where all the conditions are right for human beings to go through their evolution in freedom, his 'entry into heaven' is really an 'entry into the earth'.

We can say: With his death Christ made his way into a *triple hell* to become heaven, there, himself.

The first hell was the darkness in the consciousness of the Hierarchies regarding death. This darkness is being transformed by Christ into light. Thanks to the Christ, the Hierarchies now know what they have to do as they accompany human beings. The second descent into hell is the descent of Christ to the dead who – as Achilles tells Odysseus – experienced, without him, an actual eclipse of consciousness and a shadow existence. Christ's death is itself the descent to the dead: he brings light to their consciousness. Through him human beings are enabled to have an ego-consciousness even after death. The third descent into hell – which is called the Ascension – is the entering of the Christ into the sum total of the earth's forces and the forces of nature.

Thus the entry of the Christ into both hell and heaven has a spiritual, a soul and a bodily dimension: it is an event for the spiritual Hierarchies, for humankind and for the earth. All this is included when Rudolf Steiner's spiritual science speaks about the Christ event as a comprehensive cosmic event involving the heavens, humanity and the chthonic forces.

The Mystery of Golgotha as the Archetypal Ecological Phenomenon

The Mystery of Golgotha can in a Goethean sense be regarded as the *archetypal ecological phenomenon* in the evolution of the earth and of humankind. The Christ event shows us in an archetypal way how the Being of Love treated the earth. In the way the Christ Being handled nature we see an example for how human beings in their imitation of Christ should deal with the earth. On the one side we have the death on the cross, where his blood flows into the earth and the earth absorbs it. This flowing of the blood from the wounds of the Redeemer into the earth was accompanied by a supersensible phenomenon, the etherization of the blood of the Redeemer. This etherized blood gives the earth a new spiritual aura which contains all the forces of cosmic Love.

These forces supply the required conditions so that all the egoism that has its physical foundation in human blood may, in the course of evolution, be purified and transformed into the power of love.

This is to be taken quite literally as an archetypal ecological phenomenon. Rudolf Steiner describes it in this way. If a being from Mars or Venus had observed the earth during all the millennia before Christ, and had then observed it during the moments in which Christ was dying on the cross, it would have seen from the far distance of the cosmos an enormous transformation taking place in the aura of the earth. The earth shines forth with absolutely new colours, expressing the fact that the sum total of the forces of Love have been taken up into its aura.

During the whole second half of evolution every human being will be living within this supersensible aura of the earth. To the extent that each person unites him or herself, out of freedom, with these Christ forces, they will acquire the possibility of having a part in the selfsame purifying power that love has over egoism, the selfsame victorious power that freedom has over the force of necessity working in the blood.

The second event that belongs to this archetypal ecological phenomenon is that through the *laying of the body in the grave* the material filling of the physical body penetrated as dust into a crevice in the earth made by the earthquake. Thus the earth received the communion of Christ's body after being impregnated with his blood. Out of the empty grave there arose the purely spiritual resurrection body. All the supersensible form-forces of the human physical body as a synthesizing system of forces comprising all the form-forces of the stones, the plants and the animals are contained in the resurrection body of Christ. It is in these forces that our second ecological task lies hidden.

The first is the ecological labour of love, of purifying ourselves of all egoism through the power of love. The second task falls to thinking, to bring the whole of creation to resurrection in the Logos, to redeem it from the forces of heaviness. This will happen through human beings giving each thing a resurrection body in his own thinking. The earth will be transformed into a body of love through the over-coming of egoism and into the body of the Logos through the resurrection of the flesh in the thinking human spirit.

The Natural Order and the Moral Order Becoming One Again

Part and parcel of the cosmic nature of the Mystery of Golgotha actually becoming an archetypal ecological phenomenon is the reuniting of the natural and the moral order.

Human beings became accustomed a long time ago to experiencing these two realms as separate from each other. On the one hand we see the natural order with its immutable laws and its immutable natural forces. On the other hand we experience our inner nature—our thoughts, feelings, will impulses and ideals—as quite another thing, as a world entirely separate from the first one. Human beings think that their ideals can have no effect on nature. These cannot possibly have an actual effect like an earthquake or a storm.

The separation between the natural and the moral order is also part of the necessities of evolution. It had to be the case that a human being's moral life does not immediately affect nature. This was the only way for human freedom to be possible. For it would be quite impossible for human beings to experience the application of their forces in freedom if every thought, every feeling and every will impulse were immediately to affect nature. It is just because of the fact that our inner moral order does not directly intervene in the forces of the physical world but has at present almost no consequences other than inner ones that we can feel *free*.

This 'separation' is not an absolute one but relies in reality on a time shift. A basic difference between divine and human action—at the present middle stage of evolution—consists in divine action working directly and immediately, meaning that it is a natural effect at the moment of being a natural creation. The thoughts of godlike beings are at one and the same time deeds in the natural world. Where human beings are concerned their moral world remains *for the time being* a purely inner world. Even though human beings act on the basis of thoughts and feelings, the immediate effect these actions have on the body of the cosmos is very limited. The actual results do not appear in physical form until later.

It is just this lapse of time which makes it difficult for human beings to trace the actual causes of the physical consequences they bring about in the course of time. They have therefore got used to thinking that the world of their inner life has no effect whatever on the world of nature because they can only understand the simultaneous presence of cause and effect in the material world.

This is how an awareness of reincarnation has been lost.

For the law of reincarnation is the specifically human way of bringing the moral and the natural order into a reciprocal action in time of cause and effect. The moral life a human being creates in himself in one life is transformed, *in the next life*, into the law governing the form of his bodily nature and the external/natural reality of his karma.

Because this 'shift' in time is difficult to penetrate, human beings get a feeling of freedom in their handling of moral phenomena. However, this 'freedom' can in an actual sense only be a sort of ignorance, which then enables 'wilfulness' to come about. Wilful action is the first negative phase of freedom, and it needs to be overcome by consciously doing what is objectively necessary out of one's own free will.

Reacquiring a consciousness of reincarnation – the essential dependence of the natural order, as effect, on the moral order, as cause, even if this is for the time being drawn apart in time – is a significant prerequisite for understanding the Mystery of Golgotha as an archetypal cosmic phenomenon of the 'reuniting' of the natural and the moral order.

The bodily form in the present life is the outcome of what a human being had become morally in the previous life. This delay in time, brought about in human consciousness as the total result of alienation from nature, will be brought to synchronization again by the Mystery of Golgotha. The reciprocal alienation between human beings and nature will be revoked through everything Christ is accomplishing.

This is one of the most significant differences between human nature at the present level of evolution and godlike nature. A human being experiences the 'separation' between nature and morality and misinterprets it as an objective fact, a law of nature, instead of understanding it correctly as a fact of consciousness. For human beings to reach the 'divine' level of consciousness would mean their becoming, spiritually, so creative that their creations would be as 'natural' as those of divine beings.

The Being of Love, who is making the earth into a sun again, will reunite the godlike creativity of the sun and the earth's natural creatures. In their imitation of him human beings are imitating this cosmic reunion.

Those are no mere empty images when, in the Gospels, we are told that during the death of the Being of Love the sun became darkened and the earth quaked. The sun and the earth took an actual part in the event. The archetypal phenomenon of the moral order—the sacrifice of love—affects them directly. For it is also the archetypal phenomenon of the natural order—the resurrection of the flesh. Human beings in the course of their evolution need to understand this mystery better and better and take their part in accomplishing it. The millennia after the Christ event exist for the 'imitation' of Christ, for the bringing forth, stage by stage, of a reunification of the natural order and the moral order. The whole of creation is longing to be transformed by human love.

The Initiation in the Mysteries Becoming a Historical Fact

These thoughts on the nature of Christianity may perhaps be brought to a close by referring to another fact showing that Christianity is the synthesis and the fulfilment of all the religions of humankind.

The Christ event is a divine deed uniting and fulfilling *all the initiations of the ancient Mysteries*. Through the Mystery of Golgotha initiation was made 'public' and therefore accessible to everyone. There unfolded before the eyes of the world, as historical fact, what could take place in ancient times only in the seclusion of the Mysteries—and then only for a few chosen ones.

When the decision was reached to put Jesus Christ to death the reason for it was given out to be his betrayal of the Mysteries, for instance through the raising of Lazarus, which represented an initiation. The universal quality of the

Christ consists in the fact that all the Mysteries of initiation were made universally accessible. Everything necessary for entering the spiritual world, the initiation process, was changed into the individual task of development of each single human being, to be carried out in freedom. The deeds of Christ will become the spiritually real initiation of each individual. He dedicates the human soul to the spirit; a human being who makes himself Christian gradually enters into the spiritual essence of the whole cosmos. The hearer of the Word—the human being—himself becomes the creative cosmic Word.

In his lectures on St Mark's Gospel* Rudolf Steiner describes how part of the nature of the Mystery of Golgotha was the cosmic/godlike decision of the Sun Being to overcome all hesitation and to make the enormous resolve to carry out, as a historical fact, the initiation of the ancient Mysteries before the eyes of the whole world. The death and resurrection of Christ *is* the essence of all initiation. In this cosmic/godlike initiation is contained the totality of human evolution in freedom. In passing through death and the gravelike stillness of the physical world the human being brings forth a new, resurrected earth.

It is not he, the human being, who dies as a creative/spiritual being in the wasteland of the natural order. But the earth arises, rejuvenated and made human, in the resurrection of man.

Christ's decision to make the mystery of initiation public was first put into practice with the *raising of Lazarus*. A week later came the fulfilling of all expectations of all the Mystery Schools and all initiates. Through the suffering, the death and the resurrection of the God-imbued human being, of the God who had become a human being, the practices of all the Mysteries and of all the religions—all the paths leading back into the spiritual world—were accomplished as a

---

*See note on page 26.

historical happening in a universally archetypal form for all humanity.

This made the old initiation available to every human being through the fact that it had been made *perceptible* for everyone as a visible historical event, and therefore also *thinkable*. The Word has become flesh: the spiritual essence of all things had become visibly perceptible, so as to become the overall material and the task for human freedom of thought. Thus through the Mystery of Golgotha also initiation has been made perceptible so as to give each human being the possibility to penetrate with his thinking into the mystery of death and be capable of joining with love in celebrating, through thinking, the resurrection of all flesh. The consummation of every religion is the resurrection of man.

The incarnation of the Logos encompasses every birth — the birth of every single thing in order for it to become perceptible to human beings. The Mystery of Golgotha comprises every death as an initiation into a spiritual resurrection.

If we take into account everything that has been said up till now we can understand what Rudolf Steiner means when he says: Christianity is not one religion among others but the fulfilment and completion of all religion.

'Religion' in the actual sense of the word is the striving of human beings to reach God. The Mystery of Golgotha, however, is the answer the spiritual world brings to this religious striving of humankind to bring it to *fulfilment*.

Through the deed of the Being of Love and through the mystical fact of the Mystery of Golgotha human nature has become filled with godlike forces. The Being of Love has turned human nature into a nature of love. This has wiped out the distinction in principle between man and God. The religion of the future is man in that he takes up and carries out the deification of man and of the earth as a task of freedom and of love.

6
THE RIDDLE OF ISLAM AND THE CHRISTIANITY OF THE PAST

Contemplating the Christ Mystery has brought us to the highest pinnacle of the evolution of humankind, opening up a vista of the great ideals of the future. This makes it all the more necessary to take seriously the warning not to want to remain forever at the summit — like Peter on the mountain of the Transfiguration. What comes to us as a presentiment of a great ideal has to descend into the valleys of daily life so that this daily life may be gradually fructified and transformed in all its aspects. So let us make this descent also, and look at human life as it has actually proceeded during the two thousand years after the Christ event.

What ought we to expect when we pass from Christ's deeds to human deeds? We ought to expect human beings to be *right at the beginning* of bringing to realization what was accomplished by the Mystery of Golgotha as the overall future ideal of all endeavour. What this really means is that both where our understanding of it and also our actions are concerned human beings to begin with remained just as they were. In many people there was certainly a deeply felt spiritual presentiment — they called it 'faith' — that Christ's deeds signified human 'redemption', the great turning-point of evolution. But because they could not as yet weigh up *in their thinking* the practical existential consequences for human freedom, they accepted the redemption at first almost exclusively as Christ's 'Grace' given to those human beings who opened themselves to it.

Therefore I must also warn my readers at this point not to underestimate the inner drama that has arisen in the past two thousand years. We must not expect the evolution of religion to run its course as 'positively' *after* Christ as *before* Christ. Before Christ humanity was guided by divine Grace; after Christ human freedom became more and more important.

Both in past Christianity and in Islam there still lives a tremendous amount that belongs to pre-Christian times. This should not be condemned on the one hand in a moralizing way, by regarding it as justified by the necessities of evolution, nor should it on the other hand be covered up or played down. If we were to be guilty of this latter action it would be impossible for us to pinpoint and tackle the religious renewal so necessary today.

Freedom as the Criterion of Good and Evil

If we trace the evolution of humankind since the Christ event we become aware of the necessity of bearing in mind the essential reciprocal action of force and counter-force in the structure of evolution. The period after the turning-point of time is the time for the completing and finalizing of the *conditions* for the attainment and exercise of freedom. Freedom is only possible, however, if the totality of essential counter-forces are always present. Each force needs its counter-force in order to develop and grow strong. Divine goodness reaches its culmination, its conclusion for human beings in the completion of all the necessary conditions for their becoming co-creators. The totality of counter-forces has also to arise at the same time.

The meaning of the 'turning-point of time' in evolution — of the 'fulness of time' — is that an actual *watershed* is being crossed, even if only in a rudimentary way to start with. The reason for this watershed is in the nature of freedom itself. Where freedom is still almost non-existent evolution is guided by divine necessity. In actual fact, human beings are at this stage not yet capable of choosing between Good and Evil. Everything is still at the preparatory stage.

The fundamental character of evolution after the turning-point, however, consists in the finality that arises from the addition of human freedom and the watershed this brings about. This 'separating of the ways', which is only just beginning, will necessarily become more and more radical.

The Good and Evil in humankind will be intensified through the radicalization of the force of freedom. This means, at the same time, that *freedom* itself will increasingly be made more and more into the exclusively moral criterion of Good and Evil, Good being everything that makes human beings more free, and Evil everything that makes us less so.

The realization of freedom is, quite simply, what moral good is, in the sense that human beings make more and more actual and active the godlike forces they take into themselves. A human being will thus become more and more an ego being, more and more creative, more and more 'godlike'. This quality of godliness is the archetype of goodness for us human beings, and it is in acquiring a godlike creativity that our capacity *to be free* will become more and more real.

Evil, on the other hand, can only be understood as a failure to reach creative freedom. All external, authoritatively based criteria will become more and more obsolete. In the age of freedom one can only prove that something is evil by showing that it makes a person as such less free. This is the only basis for considering it evil. The whole of moral goodness is contained in the actual reality of freedom. Human beings have only to learn to understand freedom much more clearly on its own merits than is usually the case.

Freedom is not one human dimension among others, it is our very *being*. Anything that makes us less free makes us less 'human'. Moral evil is quite simply the loss of our humanity.

'Petrine' Christianity and Materialism

In the Gospels Christ gives one of the twelve apostles the

name 'Petrus', which means rock, stone. He represents the kind of human being who for the time being is in the process of uniting more and more deeply with the dead mineral forces of nature and becoming one with them. Christ tells this Petrus-man that he should 'follow' him immediately (John 21:22). The other apostle, the one whom the Master loved, must wait, however, until he returns.

Peter's destiny is the destiny of the first phase of Christianity, the one that immediately 'follows' the Christ event. During this time humankind is meant to sink even more deeply into materialism. This 'petrine' element has only reached its culmination now, in our time. The essence of freedom is in overcoming the determinism of nature. In order to be able to overcome materialism one must first of all have fully experienced it, otherwise one would have nothing to overcome. Therefore Christ says in advance that the culture of the 'Christian Occident' will at first have to be a culture of the 'petrine' human being.

This is telling us something else as well. Christ has come among humankind to bring about in human nature the forces enabling individual freedom to exist. Christ's activity is the polar opposite of natural activity. Natural activity functions out of necessity, excluding freedom, whereas Christ's activity is intended to make of every necessity an occasion for freedom.

In other words: the activity of the Being of Love is not forced upon us. It can only offer possibilities and awaken faculties; a human being has to take them up and exercise them in freedom. With regard to the Christ activity it is not what Christ 'does' for us but the human being's free response to it that is the determining factor – Christ merely lays the offer open. Thus the history of past Christianity is the history of the beginnings of humanity's response to the Christ Being and his activity. It is the history of the first beginnings of human freedom.

Whilst human freedom in its relation to the Being of Love

is only in its *infancy*, natural activity is not in its infancy but is pursuing its course with the *matured* forces and calculability of its natural laws. Whereas freedom is just at the beginning, natural necessity is in full swing. The element of freedom does not have to occur, one can miss out on it time and again—just because it is optional. Natural necessity has to happen, however—this cannot be avoided.

So it cannot be otherwise that in the first phase of Christianity—that of human evolution in freedom—the determinist nature of materialism will set its stamp on culture far more forcefully than will the tender shoots of freedom. But from a qualitative point of view the value of this quantitatively modest phenomenon is infinitely more valuable, and in the course of future evolution it will come into its own.

Christian or Islamic Natural Science?

With its emphasis on *necessity* in both the natural and the divine order of things Islam belongs to the very nature of petrine Christianity itself. For this kind of Christianity is far less different from the nature of Islam, in its objective reality, than is commonly supposed.

It would be a distortion of history if we were to regard Islam as the straightforward opposite of Christianity. One mould of Christianity is not the same as another. Theory is frequently different from practice. In real life, Christianity and Islam are never in opposition but only *real people* on both sides who call themselves 'Muslim' or 'Christian'. The important question is what is *living* in these people and not which 'religion' they carry around in their heads as a theory.

Therefore, in order even to be able to understand Islam, we must look less at Christian theory and more at the actual reality of petrine Christianity. The first millennium was coloured more by faith and the second millennium more by science. *Religious faith* expects everything to be the work of divine Grace, which is often considered to be no less all-powerful than in the Koran. *Natural science* has replaced faith in the omnipotence of God by faith in the omnipotence of nature, the decisive factor in both cases being the impotence of human freedom which, in the true sense of the word, is much more in keeping with the Muslim outlook than the Christian one.

The triumphs of science and the technical mastery of the physical world have caused a giddiness, an inner intoxication that has almost hypnotized modern humanity. On the other hand the scientific, materialistic West has increasingly had recourse in recent times to the ancient eastern religions, to eastern spirituality. The very nature of this, however, as we have already seen, is elusive. It can hardly be of service in overcoming materialism, in fact it frequently serves to justify it. This happens in that life runs along double tracks: on the one side a spirituality that often has hardly anything to do with real life; and on the other side the harsh world of competition and unlimited desires. Consequently the human spirit is once again impotent with respect to the material world; again we have the kind of Christianity that is much closer to Islam than to real Christianity.

Western natural science is a product of 'Christian' culture. Rudolf Steiner never tires of stressing that in reality this science comes from 'Arabism'. It arose regardless of the Christ impulse. Time and again it has regarded human freedom as an illusion. Matter was considered to be effectively the only reality. It is not the soul—let alone the spirit—which is the cause of what occurs in the body, but just the reverse, if one still speaks of soul at all.

The Arabic/Islamic character of modern natural science is shown clearly by Rudolf Steiner in his research into the reincarnation of single individuals. The same individuals who devoted all their strength and their whole enthusiasm to spreading Islam come back again, centuries later, and are the founders of modern materialistic natural science. The innermost nerve of their endeavour is exactly the same as before — in the past the almighty Allah, and now almighty nature. What both have in common is the disregard of individual human freedom.

It is so important to know that the leading scientists in the Christian West in the past centuries were the leaders who, in their previous important incarnation, spread Islam. They are the same individualities! They could not conquer Christianity in those days from outside, through war, but they are conquering it now almost imperceptibly, by hollowing it out from inside through modern materialistic science. Looked at this way the history of Christianity and Islam appears quite different from the way it is usually presented.

A New Religion After Christ?

Islam is the only religion of world significance that has arisen after Christ. From all that has been said it should be clear that where Christianity is really understood its character as a conclusion must also be understood: its absolute universalism in that the Christ Being anticipated all the future stages of human evolution. The founding of a new religion after the coming of Christ can only happen by ignoring the Christ impulse or working in opposition to it. There is no mistaking what Rudolf Steiner says about this. In his lecture given on 13 April 1922* he says:

> Through the event in which a God passed through the human fate of birth and death the earth received its meaning, and this event can therefore never be surpassed. After the coming of Christianity — and this is quite clear to anyone acquainted with the founding of Christianity — a new religion can no longer be founded. One would not understand Christianity properly if one were to believe a new religion could be founded.

---

*Published in English as *Knowledge and Initiation*, Steiner Book Centre, N. Vancouver, no date.

We have seen that the fundamental character of religion before Christ was the human *searching* to reunite with the sphere of the gods. The Christ event entirely reverses this religious phenomenon. The searching for reunion ceases to be a searching because the Godhead comes to meet humanity enabling the searching to be transformed more and more into a *finding*. Finding one's way to the Christ Being is in this sense the fulfilment of all humanity's religious searching. This fulfilment cannot be the monopoly or the possession of one culture or one person, because it represents the independent task of *every* human being. Where human freedom is no less important than divine Grace, there true Christianity arises. True Christianity is the religion of human freedom as the fulfilment of the working of divine Grace.

The Essence of Islam: Monotheism and Predestination

The very essence of Islam as a religion can doubtless be seen in its radical monotheism. The most important statement in the Koran is: 'Allah is the only God and Mohammed is his prophet.' Where Allah is presented as the only God the secondary statement is repeatedly added: 'and he has no son'. This subordinate clause can only be understood in relation to the basic statement of Christianity that the divine 'Father' sent his 'Son' into the world.

In this discussion of principle two levels must be clearly distinguished. One of them refers to what takes place within human consciousness; and everything that Mohammed as a human being perceives or thinks of Christianity also takes place on this level. All that Christians themselves have or have not understood about the Christ Being also belongs here. On this human level there were certainly many misunderstandings on both sides with regard to the Christ impulse. This is, after all, only just beginning to be active among humankind. Therefore the way the Christian Trinity was often interpreted can have presented, in Mohammed's eyes, a danger of falling back into polytheism. This may at least partly explain his unhesitating return to the uncompromising monotheism of the Old Testament.

However, the other level is that of the *spiritual beings* who are the source of the Koran's inspiration. These inspiring beings know what they intend when they inspire the statement: 'Allah is the only God, and he has no son.' These spiritual beings know what effect this statement will have on humankind; it will directly extinguish a consciousness of the Christ Being. However, this is just what they intend, otherwise they would not send this inspiration.

Therefore we can say: *Spiritual powers* have brought the Koran and Islam about in humanity, powers with the evolutionary task of offering the necessary counter-force to the true element of Christian freedom. In the one-sided emphasis on monotheistic determinism we see the expression of a spiritual will to work counter to the impulse of human freedom.

Seen in this light, the argument between Christianity and Islam is the earthly projection of the supersensible battle between Christian and antichristian spiritual beings. In the projection a great deal comes over as distorted and confused. A lot of things that call themselves 'Christian' are much more Islamic than Christian—and vice versa. The pure archetypal phenomenon of this, however, must also be sought for in the supersensible world. This perspective alone enables us to understand, for example, the heroic and temperamental nature of the battle that raged in the Middle Ages between Christian Scholastics and Arabian Aristotelianism. (More about this later.)

Mohammed, the prophet of Islam, attributes his inspirations to a spiritual being whom he identifies as the Archangel Gabriel, known to both Judaism and Christianity. In the Gospels Gabriel announces the immaculate conception of Jesus of Nazareth. From his research in the supersensible world Rudolf Steiner confirms that this archangel being does in actual fact guide all the forces of birth and of natural life according to the directions of still higher beings.

However, there were, after the coming of Christ, two opposing spiritual powers active in the forces of birth and life. This 'dichotomy' was brought about by the Christ event in all the spiritual Hierarchies. There had to come about through Christ a separation of the heavenly spirits in order to create force and counter-force in all human spheres, so that there would be a field in which freedom could be practised. Therefore in the realm of the Gabrielic beings, too, one of the forces continues to work as it did before Christ — continuing to guide all the natural forces in a way that excludes freedom. We can call it the pre-Christian Gabrielic power which continues to work in a pre-Christian way also after the coming of Christ. Mohammed is right to call this power 'Gabriel', for it represents a divinity who unfolds its all-powerful character through the forces of the *natural part of the human being.*

The other Gabrielic beings have taken into themselves the Christ impulse and the Christ activity, and want to follow Christ in shaping the forces of birth and heredity in such a way that these do not overpower human beings but empower them with freedom. This Christian Gabriel intends human beings to experience the forces of nature in a way that leaves them free, so that they can exercise their individual freedom.

A Danger of Polytheism in the Christian Trinity?

It is not easy to testify fully to the *oneness* of God when one is at the same time becoming conscious of the fact that in the evolution of humankind the Godhead works in *three* totally different ways. There is always the danger that the three different ways of working will be referred back to the being and the nature of God himself. Yet any direct statement concerning the nature of God *per se* is essentially idle speculation. No human being, even an initiate, experiences God as he is in himself, but only the way he works in *human beings*. Therefore we can understand why Rudolf Steiner is a person who least of all makes statements about the nature of the Godhead *per se*.

In his workings in the world the Godhead comes to threefold expression, firstly as *natural necessity* in all natural activity. This kind of activity can be called 'paternal' because it serves as a foundation for all other things and has to precede them. Everything of a *bodily nature* arises through this first activity. The second way the Godhead works brings about the human *soul*, the enclosed, inward nature of thinking, feeling and will which at first, however, represent pure receptivity, merely an inner image and mirroring of what is outside.

The third way the Godhead works — the actual spiritual way — is experienced by human beings through a transformation of the soul's passivity into an individual, independent spiritual activity.

The extreme monotheism of Islam excludes the Trinity, both the trinity of God's activity in the world and the human experience of it. This is bound to lead to extreme fatalism and determinism. The distinction between spirit and matter is basically abolished, because the Godhead works as all-powerfully and deterministically as nature itself. In reality natural necessity and predestination are in this case one and the same.

The Christian Scholastics and Arabian Aristotelianism

The fact that Islam represents the counter-force to the real Christian impulse of individual, human freedom can be

seen in the archetypal phenomenon of the medieval con-
troversy between Christian Scholasticism and the Islamic
Aristotelian thinkers, especially Averroës and Avicenna
who represented Arabism. In those days the great battle
was fought out in relation to the *individual immortality* of
human beings. We must come to a proper understanding of
the principle behind this confrontation between Christianity and Islam.

There are pictures showing Thomas Aquinas sitting on a
centrally placed throne with a book in his hand, and
beneath his feet—not *at* his feet—are the Arabian thinkers.
We can imagine that the book Thomas holds in his hand is
the book called the *Summa against the Heathens*, in which he
campaigns with such vigour against the Arabic/Islamic
commentators on Aristotle in particular. The mood is
unmistakable: it is not a war with external weapons, but it
is certainly a gigantic *spiritual battle* being fought with
spiritual weapons.

It is a spiritual battle for the *individual immortality* of the
human being! However, a modern person is so totally
occupied with quite different things that he cannot understand how such an odd matter—odd today—could get
people so worked up.

What was so terrible about the claims of these Arabian
thinkers? Already a long time before Thomas's time, the
authoritative Averroës had interpreted Aristotle as saying
that each human being at birth is given a drop of cosmic
intelligence—the νους (Nous)—so that it is only the one
universal divine cosmic intelligence which thinks in each
human being. When a person dies, when the bodily vehicle
decays, this drop of cosmic intelligence is absorbed again
into the whole. Therefore there can be no question of individual immortality.

This interpretation of Aristotle fits together very well
with the omnipotence of Allah; it is Allah who thinks in all
creatures and guides them. To imagine you are indepen-

dent in your thinking or your actions is pure illusion. The religious duty of human beings is precisely the duty of seeing through and overcoming this fundamental illusion. Religion consists in human beings submitting to the almighty will of Allah.

But how does it stand with regard to Aristotle himself? It is not so easy to answer this question. Aristotle was the first great thinker to whom the relationship with the body became so important for a human being's self-awareness that he advocated the idea that the entire individual human being arises at the same time as the body. Aristotle endeavoured, as opposed to Plato to a certain extent, to look for the spirit entirely within the world of matter and not separate from it.

According to Aristotle there was no such thing as a human soul which had individualized itself before birth — in previous incarnations perhaps. Neither does Aristotle present the first and only union with the body — at least not clearly — as a process of individualization of the human soul. Human immortality lies in your memory of the body you have cast aside. This, however, is a segment of the universal activity of God in nature, and contains *per se* nothing individually human. So we cannot contend that Aristotle says without any shadow of doubt that after death every human being preserves an *individual* ego consciousness — where the actual spiritual content of this ego should of course be entirely individual and unique.

But the Christian thinkers of the Middle Ages then said this to themselves. In the Averroës interpretation of Aristotle the nature of Christianity is being directly denied. Human dignity is being trampled underfoot. We only acquire our dignity from Christ, the being of the ego, because we owe it to the fact of his dwelling in us that we can experience ourselves as separate, individual ego beings each with our own autonomy. This is the only way that a human being can become a morally responsible being —

capable of Good and Evil—because he is capable of individual freedom.

The Scholastics, therefore, wanted to prove that human beings are individual, independent beings, individually accountable and responsible for their deeds and therefore also individually immortal. But it was just this point that caused the great misunderstanding, then, and still does today. If a human being as a human being *is* free, then he is free *by nature*, which means he is not free! So we see that the Christian element, the very thing the Scholastics wanted to defend, was only just beginning to take root in them as well, because they could not as yet clearly see the immanent structure of freedom in the evolutionary perspective. So we cannot sum up human freedom in any other way than by saying: Human beings can *become* free, but they are not forced to do so, otherwise they would not be free.

The Christian thinkers were saying a human being *is* free. The Islamic thinkers said a human being is *not* free. Both of them can be right. Each human being decides in the course of his actual evolution whether he is going to agree with the one statement or the other—not by proving a theory, but through what he does or does not become in his own real being.

The Struggle for Individual Immortality

Therefore it is not a question of simply swearing by or 'proving' individual immortality; it is a matter of something quite different. One has, namely, to strengthen one's individual self through actually developing one's own being, and really exercising one's ego-nature, making it so real, substantial and effective that not only in theory but out of actual experience one is justified in speaking of the kind of ego-nature that can continue to exist even without the support of the body, even after death, as an independent, individual spirit being. No human being can be more of an ego being after death than he has become in life.

There are lectures by Rudolf Steiner in which he describes the moving inner battles of the Scholastics. By day they defended individual immortality with all their strength and all their power of argument because, for them, the very essence of Christianity depended on this question. While they were asleep, or in moments of mental rapture, Averroës, who had died long since, appeared to them, however, and through his form as a dead person attempted to prove to them the opposite!

One or another Scholastic still had the ability to perceive Averroës supersensibly, as he had become after his death. He told them: A human being cannot survive after death as an independent, spiritual individuality. His thoughts disperse again into the universal cosmic intelligence. Averroës himself appeared to these Christian Scholastics and confounded their spiritual conviction by literally 'demonstrating' to them the correctness of his interpretation of Aristotle. Averroës' thoughts were indeed such a strong denial of freedom and of individual self that they left nothing individual behind after death; they had totally dispersed in the universal non-individualized cosmic intelligence.

What the Scholastics were striving to attain was insight into the fact that the meaning of repeated earth lives is that we have this lengthy evolution for the very purpose of giving our ego-nature and our individual immortality the chance of coming into being and growing more and more actual and substantial in the course of time.

If the kingdom of natural determinism functions out of necessity and if truly Christian happenings are those which take place in freedom — but are not bound to take place — then the burning question could arise: why did the spiritual guidance of humankind make special provision for a religion that emphasizes natural necessity, if from the outset the impulse of freedom has more than enough counterforce, with all the forces of nature arrayed against it?

Rudolf Steiner describes in this connection the intentions behind the magnificent Academy of Gundeshapur around

the turn of the eighth to ninth century. The great ruler
Harun-al-Rashid had gathered around him the best repre-
sentatives of eastern and Greek wisdom and art. If things
had happened according to the intentions of certain spiritual powers this cultural centre would have anticipated a
stage of evolution which the good powers planned should
happen two thousand years later, in our time.

It was a premature unfolding of what Rudolf Steiner calls
the 'consciousness soul' – and 'premature' always means
that human freedom is not a participatory factor in it.
Human beings would have made tremendous progress in
knowledge and the technical handling of the occult forces in
nature which, thanks be, are still hardly known to us today.

At this point the *good* spiritual powers intervened – those
spiritual powers whose sole wish is to guide humanity in a
way that is compatible with human freedom – and miti-
gated this dangerous impulse of Gundeshapur *by means of
Islam*. Aristotle, in his Arabian form, was Islam-ized, and
through Islam everything was made *abstract*. In this way
one of the greatest dangers in the evolution of humankind
was partly diverted.

One of the characteristics of Islamic monotheism is
spiritual abstraction. It does not think in terms of an infinite
variety of spiritual beings and nature spirits. There does not
arise out of it – in the way it was being prepared for in the
Aristotelian Academy in Gundeshapur – an exhaustive,
pragmatic *spiritual* view of nature beings and natural
phenomena. Everything is referred back to a single divine/
spiritual being: God or Allah. The tendency arises to attribute everything that happens in the world directly to him,
without further distinction.

The Existential Contradiction: 'If it is the Will of Allah...'

In lectures held in Berlin in May 1916 Rudolf Steiner speaks
of the evolutionary task of *logical contradictions*. There was a

time when human beings were not yet capable of so much as noticing contradictions let alone struggling with them. The meaning of earth evolution consists, among other things, in the fact of human beings learning to live with oppositions as an essential evolutionary impulse promoting freedom.

There is an *existential contradiction* that fundamentally covers all contradictions. It is the contradiction between the freedom of the will of God or freedom of the human will on the one hand and the essential calculability or reliability of natural events on the other.

Islam has also been endowed with an existential contradiction from the benevolent hand of God—to serve as education for a continuous evolution due to this contradiction itself. This existential contradiction comes to expression all the time even in the daily life of orthodox Muslims. For Muslims think on the one hand that everything happens with immutable necessity, whilst saying on the other hand that only those things can happen that are the free will of Allah.

Where is the *contradiction* here? It is that natural determinism and the free will of God are mutually exclusive. Something is meant by *natural necessity* which, at the present time, can in no way be decided in freedom. It is an evolutionary impulse which was imprinted at the beginning, once and for all, upon natural creation—star, plant or animal—enabling things to be calculable. Not even God is 'free' to change natural laws at will.

The will of God—the will of Allah—on the other hand, cannot be understood in any other way than as being the polar opposite of natural necessity. This kind of will presupposes *presence of mind*—the ability to decide on the basis of knowledge and not just to repeat a natural law. To be able to make an independent resolve in the present means making a new resolve *every time*, in contrast to the calculable nature of a blind natural instinct. Thus the free will of Allah is in opposition to the determinism of nature.

Where the laws of nature are concerned everything is determined; whereas the will of Allah is entirely undetermined and free. In order to be 'free' even Allah himself cannot be determined or predestined by his own nature. For his nature *is* to create freely. Looked at in this way, *nothing* happens by necessity — everything, even in nature — happens out of the freedom of the will of God.

The next question would be: if there is *one* being — Allah — whose free will is opposed to natural determinism, why *only one*? The key statement of strict Islamic monotheism says that *Allah alone* is a spiritual being with an independent creative will. But why? If Allah's compassion is being stressed, would it not be in keeping with Allah's love for human beings not to withhold from them the best he has, the free creativity of a spiritual being?

If human beings were not to have free will at their disposal, how could they be expected to have moral accountability? They would be like creatures of nature, incapable of being good or evil, because they would be unfree.

If however human beings experience free will in themselves *nevertheless* — and consider themselves capable of being good or evil, is this free will not the God-given seed within them which they can or even ought to develop further and further because this development represents the loving will of God himself?

Christians would have the opportunity — if they were really to understand their Christianity — to solve the existential contradiction *through their way of living* (for it cannot be solved merely theoretically or logically). In the Christ event three levels came together: the level of practical experience of the earthly/*bodily* realm through the Zarathustra stream; the level of the *soul* innocence of Paradise through the Buddha stream, which has its focal point in the Luke Jesus; and the level of the cosmic/*spiritual* world, which fructifies the realm of body and soul through the incarnation of the divine Sun Being.

The innocence of Paradise is the world of miracles — the world that knows no natural necessity but only 'creations out of nothingness' that only arise 'if God so wills'. The world which has become earthly knows no miracles, only natural laws and necessities. Divine nature *unites* these two worlds — the world of freedom and the world of necessity — and solves the existential contradiction in a practical way through actual evolution itself.

Jesus of Nazareth in the Koran

In the nineteenth sura of the Koran the virgin birth of Jesus is described in detail and in a most beautiful way — not the birth of Christ, but the birth of the man Jesus. Both the Koran and the Gospel of St Luke agree that this is a *virgin birth*. We are dealing with a total 'miracle', with an event that is altogether a matter of divine freedom, and which takes place solely 'because God or Allah wills it'. Rudolf Steiner explains this significant fact to the effect that divine Guidance has, in its goodness, given every Muslim, in his Koran, something like a pearl that contains the seed for a future evolution. The virgin birth of Jesus is the hope and the opening up of freedom in a religion of inexorable fatalism and determinism. Every Muslim who meditates devoutly on this sura opens himself to the world of freedom where nothing but miracles happen, nothing but virgin births, creations out of nothingness that are not determined by previous causes.

The actual words in the Koran are: (Surah 19: 'Maryam'):

16. Relate in the Book
    (The story of) Mary,
    When she withdrew
    From her family
    To a place in the East.
17. She placed a screen

(To screen herself) from them;
Then we sent to her
Our angel, and he appeared
Before her as a man
In all respects.

18. She said: 'I seek refuge
From thee to (Allah)
Most Gracious: (come not near)
If thou dost fear Allah.'

19. He said: 'Nay, I am only
A messenger from thy Lord,
(To announce) to thee
The gift of a holy son.'

20. She said: 'How shall I
Have a son, seeing that
No man has touched me,
And I am not unchaste?'

21. He said: 'So (it will be):
Thy Lord saith, "That is
Easy for Me: and (We
Wish) to appoint him
As a Sign unto men
And a Mercy from Us:
It is a matter
(So) decreed." '

22. So she conceived him,
And she retired with him
To a remote place.

23. And the pains of childbirth
Drove her to the trunk
Of a palm tree:
She cried (in her anguish):
'Ah! would that I had
Died before this! would that
I had been a thing
Forgotten and out of sight!'

24. But (a voice) cried to her
    From beneath the (palm tree):
    'Grieve not! for thy Lord
    Hath provided a rivulet
    Beneath thee;

25. And shake towards thyself
    The trunk of the palm tree;
    It will let fall
    Fresh ripe dates upon thee.

26. So eat and drink
    And cool (thine) eye,
    And if thou dost see
    Any man, say, "I have
    Vowed a fast to (Allah)
    Most Gracious, and this day,
    Will I enter into no talk
    With any human being." '

27. At length she brought
    The (babe) to her people,
    Carrying him (in her arms).
    They said: 'O Mary!
    Truly an amazing thing
    Hast thou brought!

28. 'O sister of Aaron!
    Thy father was not
    A man of evil, nor thy
    Mother a woman unchaste!'

29. But she pointed to the babe,
    They said: 'How can we
    Talk to one who is
    A child in the cradle?'

30. He said: 'I am indeed
    A servant of Allah:
    He hath given me
    Revelation and made me
    A prophet;

31. 'And he hath made me
    Blessed wheresoever I be,
    And hath enjoined on me
    Prayer and Charity as long
    As I live:

32. '(He) hath made me kind
    To my mother, and not
    Overbearing or miserable;

33. 'So peace is on me
    The day I was born,
    The day that I die,
    And the Day that I
    Shall be raised up
    To life (again),'

34. Such (was) Jesus the son
    Of Mary: (it is) a statement
    Of truth, about which
    They (vainly) dispute.

35. It is not befitting
    To (the majesty of) Allah
    That he should beget
    A son. Glory be to him!
    When he determines
    A matter, He only says
    To it, 'Be', and it is.

36. Verily Allah is my Lord
    And your Lord: Him
    Therefore serve ye: this is
    A Way that is straight.*

To this Rudolf Steiner says: And to those people who, in the
rest of their religious confession, have this terrible contradiction of predestination versus 'If God wills it', as the
Muslims have, there comes simultaneously the revelation of

---

*Translated by Yusuf Ali and published by Amana Corporation, Mary-
land, USA.

the Nathan Jesus. If they have enough developmental ability that they can eventually come to understand this, they will tell themselves: If we recognize the nature of what is revealed to us in the Koran we shall find that pre-destination and 'God willing it' merge into one.

We can summarize this by saying: Islam and traditional Christianity have been fighting each other because up till now both of them have been to a large extent *one-sided*. The Christians said: we *are* Christians, we *have* the Christ, which means we are *free*. Islam said in essence: a human being is *not* free, there is only the will of God working in man in the same way as in nature.

Both sides had not yet sufficiently understood freedom in its reality, which is neither 'included' automatically or 'excluded' deterministically but can only *arise* creatively each moment afresh. 'Whoever strives unweariedly, him shall we redeem' (Goethe's *Faust*, Part II).

Traditional Christianity and Judaism: two great one-sided creeds. Traditional Christianity and Islam: also two great one-sided creeds. Rudolf Steiner's spiritual science enables humanity to have a new future in which expectation and fulfilment do not contradict one another—as do Judaism and traditional Christianity—and in which necessity and freedom are no longer in contradiction—as in Islam and traditional Christianity.

A Mutual Challenge and Responsibility

Rudolf Steiner often presented the relation between Islam and traditional Christianity in picture form: the image of the moon vessel with the sun host upon it. The moon religion of Islam—the lunar element represents all the natural forces in which natural necessity holds sway—has throughout the centuries held the Christian world in its grip, enclosing them like a sickle moon, from Spain across Africa, Arabia and Turkey. The potential sun element allowed itself in reality to be very much influenced by this moon religion. Islamic natural science has influenced the culture of the Christian world far more than the genuine Christian element has done. In recent times even theology looks to natural science for its justification. The western world has been conditioned by natural science, and Christian religion has become more and more of a side issue in life.

The supposed power of Islam is in reality the power-lessness of true Christianity. The emphasis on determinism and predestination is nothing new; where human beings neglect freedom, all that remains is natural necessity. For this is there by necessity, whereas freedom does not have to exist. Just because it lies in our hands we can omit it.

In every instance where Christianity fails — where free will is not cultivated — there is determinism, irrespective of what it is called. Traditional Christianity has failed in the sense that it has missed out on the most important part of it: a consciousness of the divine and cosmic Being of the Christ, who brings into the world of the Father — the world of natural necessity — the forces that bring about the resurrection of the flesh, the reversal of all necessity, through the 'freedom' to turn things in the other direction.

Rudolf Steiner stresses, therefore, that a genuine Muslim can believe in more aspects of Jesus of Nazareth than many a present-day 'Christian' theologian. He can still believe in the virgin birth of Jesus as a miracle, which is beyond the realm of natural laws. Most 'Christians' have no access any more to this mystery. What Rudolf Steiner means by this is that a present-day 'Christian' ought on no account to allow himself to be arrogant where Islam is concerned. He is not saying we ought to return to the age of simple faith, but rather that this kind of faith comes much closer to the spiritual occurrence of the virgin birth than does the kind of scientific thinking that cannot grasp the objective nature of such 'miracles' at all.

Thus we can say: the present close proximity of Islam and

Christianity can be experienced as a positive, evolution-promoting *mutual challenge*. Islam is there to show traditional Christianity its own omissions as in a mirror. It is calling on Christianity to put Christianity itself into practice. It is calling on everybody not to rest content with Christian theory but to bring it into daily living.

The challenge Christianity holds for Islam is on the other hand the challenge of individual freedom. However, an effective challenge will not spring from theory about individual freedom but only from the *reality of freedom* itself, which is seen only in really free people and can produce genuine charisma.

If it is not the theory of freedom that is lacking in Christianity but to a large extent the reality of it, and if in Islam both of these aspects are lacking, who carries the greater responsibility? Surely the one who possesses the theory but does not put it into practice! Where there actually could and should be an awareness of the fact that a human being's true dignity consists of individual freedom, the moral responsibility towards humanity is far greater than where the prerequisites for appreciating freedom are still very much lacking. Therefore Christianity has a far greater responsibility towards Islam than vice versa.

The daily rubbing of shoulders between Muslims and Christians can become more and more 'human' to the extent that each human being appreciates the already mentioned distinction between religion and individuality — not only as a theory but as his own attitude towards everybody else. As long as religion is not life itself, religion itself is still a sheath. Nobody, as a human being, is a 'Muslim', and nobody, as a human being, is a 'Christian'. Everybody goes through both traditional Christianity — as one religion among others — as well as Islam, as stages of their own development. A present-day 'Christian' may have been a Muslim in his previous life and a present-day Muslim a Christian. When, in our human encounters, we shall experience not only the other person's present sheath but the immortal core of their being which passes from sheath to sheath — from religion to religion — we shall have acquired the possibility of *loving* the eternal individuality in every other person, who is destined, after the turning-point of time, to accomplish in himself the harmonizing of all the 'religions'. Thus in every encounter we have with another person we shall experience and promote the *truly human* element.

What Each Person Looks for in the Other is the Being of Love

We can at this point ask the question: What does a person who is not a Christian look for in the other person who calls himself a Christian? He looks for the reality of love in him, for every human being, in his deepest heart, is looking for the Being of Love, the Christ Being. What past Christianity experiences today in Islam, and will experience much more strongly still, stems from the fact that each Islamic person has been knocking at the door of Christendom for a very long time in an *unconscious* but real search for the Being of Love. Islam is bitterly disappointed that it has not found the Being of Love! Thus we can actually explain the aggressive attitude of Islam towards the Christian West as being due to bitter disappointment and deprivation. The true ego of these persons has searched for the human element and not found it in the place where the conditions were such that it could have been found.

Muslims, like everyone else, are looking for the Being of Love in others. And what does traditional Christianity look for when it is challenged by Islam? It also looks for what it has lost: the cosmic/divine Being of Love, the Christ.

Thus the Christians and the Muslims share this search for the Being of Love! Thanks to the dispute between Islam and Christianity an awareness is arising that what we all have in common — the search for true humanity, the search for the

Christ Being—is something much more challenging and profound than everything we do not have in common. And just because of this, great hope for the future is arising in humankind! There is the hope that both the adherents of Christianity and the adherents of Islam will learn to appreciate more and more deeply the impulse enabling the actual Being of Christ for the first time after two thousand years to be found again among humankind.

Where will the Christ actually be found again in present-day humanity? I know of only one spiritual impulse of which I can say, 'Here we find the Christ again,' and that is the spiritual science of Rudolf Steiner. In the West, where Christianity and Islam have to work out karma together in an often tragic manner, I hear a voice calling: O Muslim, O Christian, look for the Being of Love, look for the Christ Being in the place where it is to be found! Where a science of the spirit, where a consciousness of the substantiality of the spirit is refound in such a real way that, for a person who grasps this spiritual science, a real encounter with the Being of the Christ in his supersensible reappearance becomes possible. Every Christian hopes for this; it is also the hope of every Muslim.

We all share this search for the Christ and a longing to experience the 'Christ in me' and the 'Christ in thee'. What we all can have in common today is a spiritual science that is available to everyone, by means of which both the 'Muslim' and the 'Christian' can experience spiritually the return of the Being of Love. A spiritual encounter with the Being of Love who, in our time, awaits every human being in the spirit, will be capable of evoking reconciliation and love among all humankind.

Islam will represent a test for traditional Christianity for a long time to come. May it become a test of *conscience* which will purge away all unchristian elements of power-mongering and transform them into the Christian force of freedom and of love for all people.

7

THE FUTURE OF RELIGION BY VIRTUE OF SPIRITUAL KNOWING

From what has been presented it follows that religious life will in future more and more cease to be only a partial aspect of life. Religion will stop being anything else but daily life itself. Life itself will increasingly become religion.

This development will run parallel with something else; the religion of the future will become united both with a striving for knowledge and with a person's artistic endeavours.

The addition of the dimension of 'knowing' will in no way abolish what we have up to now called 'faith'. What we have wanted to describe with this word is the 'trust' we have in mysteries — in everything we cannot yet fully grasp with our thinking. The deeper and more comprehensive our knowledge of spiritual matters becomes, all the greater and more numerous will all those things become which we do not yet understand. With regard to those things the only appropriate inner attitude is and remains that of reverence and awe — in other words: faith.

Faith as a Deepener of Knowledge

As early as the first centuries of Christianity many a Church Father was known to say *credo ut intelligam*, I believe so that my understanding may become ever better and more profound, and I may grasp things more and more deeply with my thinking. They did not think of faith and knowledge as opposites, but thought that the heart with its relationship of reverential trust in the mysteries of life has to precede understanding.

Only those things which are first of all felt and venerated in the soul's depths can truly be known more and more profoundly. If one has the proper love and attitude of faith to something, then it is inherent in the dynamics of this relationship itself that the being, the reality that is loved, will become more and more deeply and objectively understood. Does it not lie in the nature of love that it becomes real love only when the objective being of the beloved is recognized? The objective goodness of the beloved being becomes known to the extent that love is activated out of this insight into the goodness of the loved one. This is the only way in which love can be love of the real, objective being of the other one. And this alone is true love.

A similar thing applies to the polarity between Grace and freedom. In the first half of the evolution of the religious activity of human beings Grace played an almost exclusive role. After the turning-point of time religion has more and more to acquire the dimension of freedom. Therefore — as I have mentioned often enough — freedom must be understood to be the fulfilment of the working of Grace. The fact that the sphere of freedom is added is not to be understood in the sense that something is taken away from the working of Grace. Grace acquires meaning and fulfilment only when freedom is really exercised.

It is always the case that Grace and love really function only when the beloved being is given the chance to be free. Just as forces of faith are affirmed and deepened through understanding and knowledge, the experience of Grace is significantly deepened through the practice of freedom. Anyone who is fortunate enough to live in the creative forces of his own spirit has a far greater respect for Grace because he is capable of putting into practice a greater amount of that capacity for which Grace qualifies him. To be able to live in freedom is an infinitely greater grace than can be imagined by anyone who has to live without freedom.

Analogous with this we can also envisage another polarity: the polarity between freedom and love. Just as divine love precedes human freedom, human freedom on the other hand precedes love in the sense that only a person who acts entirely voluntarily, who does in freedom what he wants to do, is really capable of love. In the case of actions arising under compulsion or out of mere duty, love is not possible.

Therefore we must not conceive of freedom and love as mutually exclusive opposites but as polarities where one serves to strengthen the other.

There is something similar with regard to the polarity between individuality and community. The individual element is gradually *added* to group nature. The predominant feature of evolution before the turning-point of time was that human beings were embedded in and carried by a community. The fundamental character of the second half of evolution, where the religion of man and of everything belonging to human nature altogether arises, where everything contributing to human wholeness is experienced in a religious way, is that individual experience, experience of the unique and particular quality that each human being possesses as a distinctly different individuality, is *added* to communal experience.

Again, this experience of individuality is not in opposition to group-soul nature, rather it is a fulfilment of it. Group soul nature becomes true human community by serving the arising of unique individualities. True community as distinct from mere group-soul nature is no longer only a monotonous sameness; it is the kind of wholeness and communal possession that can only arise out of the manifold nature of individuals when each one contributes something quite different to the communal whole. The community arises where each single person carries moral responsibility for the full unfolding of the individuality of each one.

So true community is an entirely new stage of group-soul nature. The name community can in a real sense only apply where everyone experiences the particular and unique contribution of each single one. This alone makes it possible for community to be experienced as the product and fulfilment of singleness in multiplicity.

Again to the Question: What is Christian 'Transubstantiation'?

Let us turn once again to the Christian mystery of transsubstantiation, the central mystery of Christianity. Transubstantiation means that the entry of the Sun Being into the evolution of humankind and of the earth makes possible a change from the sole mastery of natural necessity to the practice of freedom. Through the exercising of freedom natural necessity will be revoked.

That in course of time a liberation from the law of natural necessity can occur in everything belonging to the natural order of things, and can bring about a transformation into the spiritual substance of the nature of freedom, would be such a momentous process that it presupposes that human beings also accomplish a transformation of their own being.

Prior to transubstantiation a human being experiences himself as a thinking spiritual being to whom the material world, the content of perception, is more 'substantial' than the spiritual. That is the point of departure of everyone nowadays, the position in which we find ourselves in our normal thinking. We are convinced that everything that is physically perceptible is real. Prior to transubstantiation, prior to the turning-point of evolution, everything exists to the extent that the physical/material world is more substantial, in our experience, i.e. more effective and causative than the spiritual element.

Christian transubstantiation, as the essential quality of religious practice, meaning inner reversal and 'conversion', becomes an experience when *man himself* as a spiritual being becomes a person's religion, and our own religious endeavour is aimed at making way for our whole being, and everything belonging to it, to become spiritual substance.

This inner transubstantiation is accomplished first of all in thinking. A human being practises grasping in thought the supersensible, essentially spiritual nature of things in such a way that, whereas previously in his experience of thinking it was matter that appeared substantial and real, he now grasps the supersensible element through intuitive and creative thinking—not as an empty postulate but as a real inner experience of self, substantial and real in the highest sense.

In his thinking spirit itself he experiences such substantiality and causality that he is able to say: In reality the spiritual element is the only thing that has substance! Matter is absolutely insubstantial and unreal, and is actually only a phenomenal and transient appearance of something spiritual, for the purpose of giving human beings the means to exercise their capacity to see the deceptive nature of it and discover for themselves, creatively, the spiritual substantiality of the cosmos.

This is the sense in which creative thinking itself becomes the greatest religious practice exercised by human beings, the greatest religious responsibility. It is only through experiencing this intuitive thinking that a human being becomes a spiritual being and acquires reality as a spiritual individuality. The coming into being of the real spiritual individuality of a human being is in fact what religion and holiness are, altogether: it is the thing which calls for the greatest reverence and veneration in the whole of human evolution. This, above all else, is justified in making a person pious.

Karma and the Task of 'Reverence for One's Self'

Similar reflections can be made concerning a second aspect in the transition of religion from traditional Christianity to its new form, to future Christianity as the religion of humankind, namely, the aspect of *reincarnation and karma* with regard to Christianity itself.

When Christ's activity is seen to be the reversing of the Father activity, inasmuch as natural necessity is transubstantiated into the real exercise of freedom, and this is actually experienced as such, then we can also grasp the activity of the *higher ego* in each single human being in all its objectivity. In this instance we experience the other aspect of the religion of man, namely, the reverence and veneration for the higher self in every human being, for this higher ego is active on behalf of the individual just as the universal Christ Ego is active on behalf of the whole of humankind. There then arises the fourth kind of religious reverence, of which Goethe speaks: *reverence for oneself.*

So let us ask: in what way is the higher ego active in karma and in reincarnation? Before one is even born the higher ego plans the main events and happenings of life, also the blows of fate signifying demands and challenges for the 'lower ego', i.e. opportunities for its further progress.

Through its connection with the body human consciousness is eventually blotted out and becomes what we call 'normal consciousness'. The future of Christianity, as the religion of everything altogether human, will increasingly consist in each person endeavouring to make his own higher ego—as a member of the Christ Ego—into his own religion, the object of his own daily veneration, until he sees his own karmic situation the way it is seen by the higher ego—as a moral intuition of love, as his own moral imagination arising for the benefit of his own and everybody else's further positive development.

The moral intuitions of one's own higher ego come to expression in all the aspects of one's daily karmic situation. Taking these seriously becomes religious practice and training. The karma-will of the higher ego is taken up into one's own liberated consciousness in such a way that one understands more and more clearly why one or another thing happens to one. The karmic situation which, without this religious/intuitive veneration of one's own higher self, was experienced solely as cause, as an unavoidable fate that one has to follow, is affirmed and willed as a positive evolutionary challenge.

Karmic circumstances are no longer experienced as extraneous necessity in the same way as natural law. One begins actually to experience the force of the higher ego in oneself and to regard the karmic situation as something that one has chosen for oneself in freedom. One no longer experiences oneself as the effect of one's karma but as its undisputed cause. One *was* free with regard to choosing what is now happening to one, and one *is* also free with respect to what one makes of it for the future.

A person who does not reverence the primal religious element, his own higher ego, nor experiences it consciously, is irreligious. A person becomes religious to the extent that the godlike being in him becomes conscious of itself and takes over the moral responsibility for its own further evolution. For this evolution is at the same time the best way of promoting the evolution of all other beings.

'Holy Scripture' as Self-discovery

I should like to mention a third factor in this connection: the relation to Holy Scripture. The future religion of humankind as a renewal and transformation of traditional Christianity will give a more and more universally human shape to everything that is initially not yet experienced in an entirely universal way. Human beings will take up the kind of relation to Holy Scripture through which it will be experienced as having been written both for everybody and for each single person. It should no longer be regarded as the Bible of any particular religion. Through spiritual science the kind of understanding of the Bible will be possible which is convincing where everyone is concerned. What has to be overcome is the sort of interpretation of the Bible that could not even do justice to the traditional text itself, for the actual nature of the text only becomes clear when it is interpreted in a wholly universal way.

As an example of this we could take the two great milestones of the Christ event: the entry of the Sun Being into the whole gamut of forces belonging to the bodily nature of man and of the earth—presented in the baptism in the Jordan and in the threefold temptation—and Gethsemane, the scene on the Mount of Olives where the body is discarded through the experience of death, and the Christ Being goes forth again into the spiritual world to enter the whole gamut of the earth's forces in a new, spiritual way.

Initially these images were regarded in traditional Christianity as the special possession, the particular images of the Christian religion, as one religion among others. However, a spiritual science in keeping with our present time ought to give every single person the possibility of not taking it in a strictly denominational way but on the basis of the kind of *self-discovery* and self-experience which is direct and accessible to everybody.

In very fact, in the case of everyone who works with sufficient energy at his own development, there arises sooner or later in his imaginative vision a picture similar to the images in the Gospels of the threefold temptation and Gethsemane. Every human being can perceive these images supersensibly in real imagination. Each person has his own experience of the fact that the Gospel writers did not present these two scenes because they were specifically

'Christian'. They can be 'seen' and experienced by every human being, irrespective of which religion he grew up in or practises.

The Gospel writers themselves, in the process of their initiation, arrived at the corresponding stages and saw with spiritual vision what every human being can also perceive in a similar way at the same stage of development. No human being has been able to perceive *with his physical senses* these two scenes in the life of Christ, for they are specifically two scenes that occurred when the Christ was alone.

As we know, it is stressed in the Gospels that he undergoes the three temptations in the wilderness; nobody was there who could have seen it with physical eyes. And on the Mount of Olives, in the Garden of Gethsemane, only three are present who, however, constantly 'fall asleep'. Christ repeatedly withdraws from them. This experience also occurs in solitude, where there is nobody else who could perceive it with their external eyes.

If one interprets the language of the Gospels correctly, one could, of one's own accord, realize that in these examples it is not primarily a matter of scenes which were witnessed historically, but of the presentation of initiation occurrences well known in the ancient Mysteries.

Every religious person of the future will be able to experience these happenings as something belonging to humankind universally, for every human being will have the chance to experience them. Everyone of us who has undergone the necessary inner development will be able to see these scenes for himself with astral vision, imaginatively. He will then well understand, *from his own experience*, that the Gospels are simply presenting stages in the evolution of every human being.

To the extent to which spiritual science enables Christianity to be more and more deeply understood, we shall grasp more and more clearly that it lies in the very nature of

Christianity not to be one religion among others but simply the religion of human beings and humankind altogether.

However, we must at the same time point out that the *words* 'Christianity', 'Christ' or 'Christian' are not the important part, for it is not a matter of words. We could use quite different terms, for the crux of the matter is to pass through the words to the actual realities.

The Future of Christ's 'Return'

These matters bring us to another aspect of the future of religion and of the religious element in humankind: to the distinction between the first and the *second coming* of Christ. The second coming is traditionally called the 'Return'. Rudolf Steiner claims that in the twentieth century we are experiencing the actual beginning of the reappearance of Christ. At the present stage of the evolution of human consciousness human beings will, from this century onwards, be able actually to experience the spiritual reappearance of Christ of which Holy Scripture also tells.

This presents us with the conscious task of grasping the essential distinction between the first coming of the Christ—his incarnation on the physical plane which happened two thousand years ago in Palestine—and the second coming, which will not take place physically any more. The reappearance is happening in the supersensible world; Christ is coming 'in the clouds of heaven', as it says in the language of the Gospels. He will come in the 'etheric world', in 'etheric form' to say the same thing in spiritual-scientific terminology.

We can say: the first coming is related to the reappearance in the same way as the Son is related to the working and the experiencing of the Holy Spirit. Christ himself distinguishes these two activities very strongly. In his final speeches in the St John's Gospel he emphasizes that he will have to depart, otherwise the Holy Spirit will not be able to come. What he says is that the way in which the Christ works and the way the Holy Spirit is experienced are not one and the same.

The activity of the Son is the working of love; it takes place in the same way for everyone. The first coming is the deed of Christ's love, which he accomplished for every-body. The experiencing of the Holy Spirit — the reappear-ing — consists on the other hand in the individual attitude of each human being towards the Being of Love and his activity. The Holy Spirit is the individualized Christ, deepened and intensified in man's inner being. Christ then begins to speak differently in each person. Goodness begins to be something different for everyone.

Through experiencing the Holy Spirit and the second coming, each human being will become a unique member of humankind. Just as the Holy Spirit is the individualized experiencing of the Christ — the experience of a deepening and intensifying of a human being's ego-nature — in a similar way the experience of the reappearance is an experiencing of the Holy Spirit; it represents an event of human consciousness, of a person's inner experience.

The reappearance of Christ occurs when human beings raise their consciousness to the Christ. I have repeatedly pointed to the fact that the Greek word translated as 'reappearance' — παρουσια = parousia — does not mean coming again or coming back. By translating it as 'return' the mistaken idea is created that the Christ had gone away, withdrawn from humanity, and is now coming back. On the contrary, the word parousia means being there, a spiritual presence. What is new about the 'reappearance' is not that the Christ himself is coming back, but that the human being in his spirit is 'coming back towards him' and experiencing his spiritual presence in a spiritual way. Human beings are now beginning actually to experience the Christ who has, all the time, been accompanying us with his spiritual presence. It is not the Christ who has 'withdrawn' from human beings but human beings who have 'withdrawn' from the Christ.

When we realize that with the first coming the deeds of Christ were the important factor, and that with the second coming the important factor must now be a human being's answer out of the freedom of conscious knowing, we can say: it is actually not possible to have an experience of the reappearance without a totally new stage also being attained in the evolution of human consciousness itself.

The spiritual science of Rudolf Steiner belongs essentially to this new stage in the development of humanity's thinking and consciousness. It is like a full-scale organ for cognizing the reappearance, a prerequisite for experiencing it consciously. We can recognize the fact that working with Rudolf Steiner's spiritual science is a gradual coming to experience the reappearance or spiritual presence of the Christ.

In this way the whole experience of Christ's reappearance becomes at the same time the new, modern stage of humankind's religion. Each individual person today experiences religion in a modern way to the extent that the spiritual presence of the Christ, an encounter with the resurrected and living One, becomes his own spiritual experience.

Christ then ceases to be a mere theory to us. Religion ceases to be the kind of abstraction which cannot sufficiently enter our actual life. To live in the spiritual presence of the resurrected Christ becomes a religious experience of the very deepest kind and sets its stamp on every human encounter and social action. Daily life itself is made into a religion; nothing is profane any more. Everything is hallowed and holy. Everyday social life becomes a perpetual sacrament.

The Religion of the Lord of Karma

Part and parcel of this happening in the realm of human consciousness—the event of the reappearance of Christ as the beginning of a universal religion of humankind—is the spiritual fact that as human beings become aware of the spiritual presence of the Christ Being he makes them able to relate to him as the 'Lord of Karma', as Rudolf Steiner calls him.

Only since the twentieth century have the evolutionary conditions for human consciousness been such that Christ can take on his office as the 'Lord of Karma'. The religion of humankind will in the future consist of each human being experiencing more and more intensely that Christ is the Lord of Karma.

'Christ is becoming the Lord of Karma' means that humankind is called upon to become the spiritual body of Christ in a more and more real way. Each human being evolves further by experiencing himself in a more and more real and actual way as an organ of the entire organism of humankind, by experiencing ever more deeply that humankind is one organism, his own organism.

This reincorporating of everyone into one organism as the overcoming of the splitting-up caused by egoism is the actual 'redemption' of humankind—the actual experiencing of the spiritual body of humankind as the religious life and sacredness of the highest order altogether.

Then *humankind* itself will become a person's religion in the sense that each human being will experience all the other human beings in such a religious and reverential way that he would like to become one with them—as an organ of his own organism. Religion will then be experienced through the utter impossibility and inability to be happy without everyone else being happy.

A human being will stop altogether wanting an advantage for himself at the expense of others. He will realize that it is an illusion to want to benefit himself by prejudicing other people, or the other way round — that something that genuinely profits other people could harm him.

To the extent to which humanity in its totality is experienced by individual human beings in spirit as one universal organism, human beings will also experience the Christ as the spiritual, universal ego of this organism. The actual experiencing of the Christ in the etheric sphere as the spiritual Lord of the karma of humankind consists in this.

Seen in this light the encounter with the 'reappearing' Christ is the start of the reuniting of all human beings with one another. This happens to begin with in consciousness, in the form of concepts which then gradually also enter into and transform daily life. Each person will then help everyone and begin to experience and to treat everyone else as belonging to himself.

This process of the building of the spiritual body of the Christ as the future of the religion of all peoples also means that a spiritualization of all matter will become more and more actual.

Why 'Spiritual Science'?

At the beginning of the twentieth century a modern *science of the spirit* arose in humanity for the first time. This fact is at the same time the start of a new stage in the religion of humankind. The 'reconnection' to the divine sphere now happens not only by means of the power of faith but increasingly through the power of cognition.

'Faith' is always connected with a group element — linked to a people, a culture or a church, to one or another authority that one 'believes in'. Knowledge as such can only be acquired individually. The new stage of religion through cognition of the supersensible element of the world will be accessible to every individual as such, and is therefore also universal.

When a scientific knowledge of the supersensible element is taken up — meaning a knowledge of it based on an individual, independent approach — then 'religion' as the relation to the divine/spiritual sphere becomes at the same time an evolutionary perspective of the *human being* himself as a cognitive and therefore *spiritual being* who can also act out of his individual autonomy of spirit in an increasingly creative and morally accountable way.

At the same time this means that the future of religion lies in the further development of the human being himself and the religion of the future can only be man — fostering all the evolutionary possibilities the gods have given him.

In future times the human being will develop a stronger and stronger religious attitude towards what is human. He bears within him the religious longing to experience an ever deeper reverence and devotion to the mystery of *man*. He will carry a more and more heartfelt and individual moral responsibility where this archetypal mystery is concerned.

But how will human beings themselves — every human being — become an example of the harmonizing of all the religions? They will become this by drawing into themselves all the different religions that they have themselves experienced one after the other and which were before the turning-point of time guided by God, and now deepen and intensify them and make them their own. What they experienced in succession and received as Grace from outside will now, through their own spiritual cognition, be joined into one whole and become, in an inwardly creative way, the integrated spiritual being of man himself.

At first, before the turning-point of time, each human being has been, consecutively and one-sidedly, a Buddhist, Hindu, Zarathustrian and Jew. And, after the turning-point of time, so long as the inner, individual turning-point has not been achieved, he will, in a similarly one-sided way, have been a Christian or a Muslim. The turning-point always comes about in such a way that the individual human being grasps all the religions, through his spiritual knowing, as aspects of what is human, and aspires, by overcoming the one-sidedness of each of them, to form them into an integrated whole within himself. The 're-ligions' belong to the limitations we have experienced in our past, and represent an inner capacity enabling us to unite them in our own being. 'Religion' is the future task of becoming universal, for which we have acquired the evol-utionary potential thanks to experiencing all the religions in succession.

Therefore the unity of all religions is understood quite differently in Rudolf Steiner's spiritual science than for example in the kind of 'comparative study of religion' very widespread today. This comparative study of religion, as already mentioned, goes in the direction of saying that when we look at the fundamental truths, at the basic statements of all religions, they all actually say the same thing. This is what is seen as the unity of the religions.

Religion as 'Self-development'

The perspective from which Rudolf Steiner's spiritual science views these matters is totally different in the sense that it is less concerned with what a particular religion says, what dogmatic or theoretical statements it contains, what truths it announces. The essence of a religion is not seen in what it 'says' but in the actual effect it has on people. The essence of a religion consists in what a person *actually becomes* through practising it.

Seen from this perspective it is of less importance that all religions 'say the same', for they arose one after another for the very reason that they should *work* in a different way, that each should have quite a *different effect* on the people concerned. The task of each religion was to awaken absolutely new and different forces in human beings.

If we reduce the religions to what their various teachings have in common we are going the best way to making religion an abstract theory that has nothing to do any more with practical daily life. In Rudolf Steiner's spiritual science, however, the unity of religions is seen as a *practical task of life* in the sense that each single person has to work every day at his or her transformation. The synthesizing of all religions is not a search for an abstract common theory but the actual and real work every single person does on himself.

If each religious stage has been a piece of actual development along the path to becoming human, then to actually unite the religions is to become fully human. This means at the same time that each religion remains incomplete and unfulfilled so long as human beings do not actually 'integrate' them all in the universal abundance of their own self-development.

Only within a person's own nature and through his own efforts can all religions become 'one' and 'agree' among themselves. The fulfilment of each religion is the actual integration of all of them in a human being's own self-realization. All religions become 'real' through actually integrating into an organism, just as each human being becomes real when he integrates into the organism of humankind as a whole. Neither of these integrations is a matter of theory; they both depend on actual inner transformation.

Nowadays a person is practising a form of religion that is right for our time if he endeavours to experience and develop his own humanity as universally as possible. The enriching of his humanity becomes the religious vocation he puts into practice in daily life. The present form religion takes is daily work on oneself, constituting a 'religion of freedom and of love'. The human being himself is the religious ideal of what each person is privileged to become in reality through constant inner transformation and

THE FUTURE OF RELIGION

development. The Christ Being is to be understood in the following way: not only in theory but in actual fact he has demonstrated and accomplished the fulfilment of everything that each of us human beings is called upon to become through the actual transformation of our own being. The 'exclusive position' of the Christ Being and of the Christ event consists in its being the one and only factor that does not permit of being 'exclusive'. It is from every possible point of view the all-embracing fulfilment.

Divine and Human Trinity

According to what has just been explained we can also look at the future of humanity's religion with the help of a totally new way of experiencing the Trinity. The Trinity of the Godhead becomes a more and more real religious experience by being actually experienced in the *human trinity*.

The membering of the human being into body, soul and *spirit* is of fundamental importance to Rudolf Steiner's spiritual science. Even his book *Theosophy* is based on this threefold distinction. It opens the way to a profounder experience of the Trinity in that we regard the divine Father principle as at work in everything of a bodily nature, the divine Son in the soul element, and we relate the Holy Spirit to the way in which a human being experiences himself as an individual spiritual being.

Thus the Trinity of the Godhead becomes the very experience whereby a human being *experiences himself* in three different ways. This is another example of a religion becoming thoroughly universal through becoming thoroughly 'human'.

So the religion of the future will increasingly consist in human beings experiencing the divine/spiritual element in an ever more real way in that they experience body, soul and spirit in their own being.

The inability to experience the Father in the physical world—atheism—arises, according to Rudolf Steiner, through the fact that human beings bear in their *physical body* the overall effect of the sickness of the Fall. They experience the effect of the activity of matter so strongly in their souls that they can no longer recognize the spirit—the spirit of the divine Father—in matter. They deny God and become atheists. Rudolf Steiner calls this tragedy an 'illness of the soul'.

A 'misfortune for the soul' is what he calls the experience of the inner self in which human beings do not encounter the Christ in their souls. This is an experience inherent in the human soul as such and not in its relation to the body. Because of this, human beings do not reach the point of overcoming sin in themselves. They do not go through the process of redemption.

Just as the divine Father is experienced in our relationship to bodily space, the Son is experienced in the overall relationship of a human being to evolution in time. Progressive evolution in time consists in the reversal of sin through redemption. The actual accomplishment of the fullness of time at the middle point of evolution gives each human being the possibility of daily inner transformation. It is only through this inner experience of transformation that the human soul acquires the opportunity at all to encounter and experience the presence of the cosmic Son, the Being of Love.

The third form of anti-religious behaviour arises when the soul does not experience its relation to the element of pure spirit. It remains merely soul, imprisoned in the group-soul element, passively supported and directed from outside. The soul is then reluctant to make the effort to actively experience the freedom and creativity of the human *spirit*, which is acquired through intuitive thinking.

Neglecting to transform the soul into something spiritual through the activation of freedom is what Rudolf Steiner calls 'soul deception'.

The soul deceives itself in that it would like to believe that it is impossible to be active and that 'freedom' is an illusion. Anything the soul does to prove that freedom is a delusion belongs to this soul deception, whereby the human soul misses out on a real experience of the Holy Spirit, the divine Spirit. The dogma of all-pervading determinism is set up also where the human being is concerned, and the freedom of the spirit declared an illusion.

The human being is then experienced solely as an effect and never as a cause, whereas the experiencing of the Holy Spirit comes about when the soul pulls itself together to reach the creativity of the human spirit.

Accordingly, the threefold religion of the future can be summarized as follows: the encounter with the Father is the overcoming of *atheism* as an illness of the soul; the encounter with the Son is the overcoming of *egoism* as soul misfortune; and the encounter with the Holy Spirit is the overcoming of *materialism* as soul deception.

This threefold self-mastery is the future of the religion of humankind, in fact the future of humankind altogether, because in the encounter with the cosmic Father, the cosmic Son and the cosmic Spirit human beings find their own true, human dignity.

By bringing forth and experiencing true humanity in himself in a more and more actual way a human being will become the sum of religious experience within himself. He will also experience the being of every other person quite simply as the substance of religion. What people will share together will be the helping of one another to overcome the three obstacles of atheism, egoism and materialism. Each person will actually be able to experience more and more clearly the presence of the divine Father, the divine Son and the divine Spirit in the other person and in himself.

From the Mystical to the Chymical Wedding

Seen in this light the future of humanity's religion consists in the esoteric dimension of religion being newly discovered and newly acquired. A true esotericism of the future will arise whenever religion is no longer experienced in a human being's abstract inner life, in abstract thoughts, feelings and will impulses, but where a real communion is experienced with *real spiritual beings*.

In the Middle Ages there was on the one hand a *mystical wedding*, which many saints aspired to, and there was also a *chymical wedding*, which was striven for more particularly in the esoteric tradition of Christianity.

The *chymical wedding* was less frequently practised in traditional Christianity because initially in this sphere of Christianity people could not muster the forces to experience the spiritual element in so real a way that not only in their own inner nature did a 'mystical wedding', an inner soul union with the divine element occur, but also through the transformation of matter a 'chymical wedding' would take place.

A universal religion of humankind only arises where each human being takes on a growing responsibility for the religious task of liberating the bodily part of the cosmos, all the nature spirits, by means of an ongoing *chymical* wedding. The resurrection of the flesh will be celebrated by spiritualizing the earthly body. There will arise a new earth and a new humanity. This *opus magnum* is the great work of the religion of all people and the whole of the future. A religious human being will become the priest and the white magician who actually performs the transubstantiation of creation.

From Being a Hermit of the Earth to Becoming a Citizen of the Cosmos

There will be a renewal of religion, and human beings will experience a new feeling for it, when the *Spiritual Hierarchies* — the angels, archangels, time spirits, spirits of form, wisdom and movement, Thrones, Cherubim and Seraphim — become a *reality* for them again. They will perceive and know them, they will move among them and hold spiritual commune with them. They will receive inspirations from them and experience their love.

Nature spirits, elemental spirits, will become approachable once again, as they were to the ancient Celtic and Germanic peoples, who experienced them as the radiant figure of Baldur, though they did not as yet have this experience out of their own freedom. Baldur died in the twilight of the gods; it is now up to us to awaken Baldur again in our own being. Through spiritual knowledge human beings will open up an approach, in freedom, to the spiritual beings at work in nature, who are waiting to be liberated by human beings from the transitory world of sense-perceptual form. From being earth hermits, human beings will again become citizens of the cosmos.

Communing with the *dead* also belongs to an actual experience of the supersensible realm as the future form of religion. The so-called 'living' will begin to take the so-called 'dead' seriously enough for a real connection, a real intercourse to come about with the dead. Dialogue with the departed will become for those left behind a most profound form of religion whereby they can experience the deepest reverence and piety.

A religious human being will seek and receive with religious thankfulness the advice of the deceased. He will willingly follow their counsel, being aware that those who are living in the spirit see the things of the world more clearly, having stripped off the egoism of separateness that necessarily results from a union with the body, and are capable of communicating divine wisdom to his thinking and his heart in a pure form.

Thus the future of religion will only come about when *daily life* itself becomes the true and profoundest religion. The distinction, in fact the separation between *sacred* and *profane*, between *holy* and *not holy*, will be revoked. The separation between the sacred and the profane spheres of life will be overcome in the same way as will the separation between the natural order and the moral order. Everything will become holy because everything will have become hallowed by human beings. Everything will become part of humankind's sacred undertaking to become truly human.

From the Hidden to the Open Temple of Humankind

The future shaping of the social sphere, the task that Rudolf Steiner calls the *threefolding of the social order*, is the whole task of the *religion* of humankind at the present time. The shaping of our social togetherness is the universal religion of the future.

It will become less and less possible to experience religion in separate temples, churches and cathedrals. Religion will in the future be experienced out-of-doors in the temple of humankind. The coming together of human beings will be held sacred. An encounter with another person will be healing and sanctifying; it will become a daily sacrament of inner transformation and communion. The threefolding of the social order is the threefolding of humanity's religion — the threefolding of the manner in which every human being is helped to become more and more human. I can here only give a quick glimpse of this religious dimension of the threefold social order.

In one sphere of life, in the realm of the *independent human spirit*, the stress is on recognizing and appreciating the unique individuality of every single human being. The appreciation of a person's individuality is the first religious experience to be put into practice by a human being of today. A modern person can only come into his own and become religiously minded through cultivating a cognition of the spirit. Only by becoming a spiritual knower does a human being experience his own creative, individual freedom, experience himself as a spiritual being in the company of other spiritual beings. Therefore the cultivation of *spiritual science* is essential for really experiencing the dignity of human individuality as a most religious force.

This freedom of cultural life is experienced particularly in the fact that each single person has the capacity to make a *judgement* about every phenomenon and every aspect of life. To cultivate one's own individual capacity to form judgements and to help everyone else to become capable of passing judgement in every sphere of life will become the true religious task of one person with regard to another.

The most religious experience possible will be the awareness that each person is being helped to experience him or herself as a free, creative individuality capable of forming their own judgement. This will happen through the pursuit of real spiritual knowledge. Although nobody can be a 'specialist' in every domain of life, we are nevertheless called upon to be competent to develop judgement about anything.

The polar opposite of this freedom governing all cultural life, where each person becomes a knower in the spirit, is the mystery of love. In an interaction of mutual help and sharing arising in the practice of *brotherliness* the important thing in economic life is to put at one another's disposal the material tools, the means and conditions necessary for life.

The religion of social life is experienced in this realm in such a way that each human being makes the other feel so reverent and devout that a genuine social *common understanding* is possible between one person and another.

Human encounter will be borne along on the wings of common interest. Taking an interest in the other person will be experienced as a liturgical service; each human being will 'serve' the divine being in the other.

Each person will experience a burning interest in how he can help the other person. By means of this interest he will want to understand the other person's individuality so that he can lovingly place at his disposal all the requirements necessary to equip him to pursue his own development. This is how a community of mutual help and brotherliness will arise.

And the third thing: the search for *balance* between the religious element of the free individuality and the religious element of the brotherliness of the community will become the religious experiencing of *equality* of all people where everybody is 'equal' in their human dignity. The dignity of a human being as such is quite simply made into everybody's religion. Each person will experience religion through the fact of resolving not to value anything more highly than each person's progressive humanness. Thus man's divine calling will become our daily religion, the religion of our social life. Human dignity is inviolable — the holy of holies in human beings before which all the angels bow down in reverence. Why should we human beings not bow down before it too?

From Tolerance of Religion to a Religion of Tolerance

Human dignity is experienced in particular through freedom of thought and of religion. A third thing must be added to the ability to form judgements and to the capacity to take an interest in other people, and that is *tolerance*. True tolerance should arise from the way each human being encounters the other:

Each person allows his neighbour full freedom in the

creating of his own religious life. Each of us has the same standing in that each one of us creates our own relation to the spiritual world in full freedom. Everyone rejoices over the fact that there is an infinite variety in the individual forms of religion, religious practice and religious life. This inner tolerance will enable a true balance to come about in humanity's sphere of individual *rights*, where the dignity of each single human being, as the most highly prized and revered treasure, is carried in each person's heart as the deepest mystery.

True tolerance will become the foundation for a new stage of religion, for tolerance will release forces with the aid of which each human being will make his own individuality more pure and complete. This most religious of treasures, embodied in the true individuality of each person, is, on the other hand, of greatest benefit to other people. All the forces that come to expression in a unique way in every individuality flow back into the totality of the organism of humankind. They benefit everybody, coming to expression in the mutual support and co-operating of everyone.

Therefore we can say: future religion will be a religion of absolute *tolerance*, of the greatest, deepest *interest* of one person in the other, and the *power of judgement* of every single individuality in all areas of life.

The religion of the future will unfold in the temple of social life, where each human encounter is experienced as a true sacrament, the ritual of which will be daily life itself, and daily life itself will become a true cult.

With the *threefolding* of the social order there will arise on the one hand the true recognition of individuality in the freedom of cultural, spiritual life and, on the other hand, real love and mutual help in the community through brotherliness in economic life. The equality of all human beings in the balance between individuality and community will be experienced through true tolerance.

The religion of the future will indeed transform human

beings from being earth hermits to becoming citizens of the cosmos; through knowledge of the spirit they will live in deeper and deeper communion with all spiritual beings.

The religion of the future will transform us from being at variance with one another to being supportive of one another through the love of each person's godlike being which is longing to be awakened to ever new life through the performance of daily divine service.

This is how religion unites with science and becomes spiritual science, a wisdom and a way of life in the most comprehensive sense. It unites with art and becomes the art of life in the broadest sense, namely, in the transformation of the social organism. Thus religion becomes both the science and the art of human beings and of everything human — the eternal art of bringing all of creation to become human and everything human to become divine.